MOVING UP WITHOUT
LOSING YOUR WAY

Moving Up without Losing Your Way

The Ethical Costs of Upward Mobility

Jennifer M. Morton

PRINCETON UNIVERSITY PRESS

PRINCETON AND OXFORD

Copyright © 2019 by Princeton University Press

Published by Princeton University Press
41 William Street, Princeton, New Jersey 08540
6 Oxford Street, Woodstock, Oxfordshire OX20 1TR

press.princeton.edu

All Rights Reserved

LCCN 2019937194
First paperback printing, 2021
Paperback ISBN 9780691216935
Cloth ISBN 9780691179230

British Library Cataloging-in-Publication Data is available

Editorial: Peter Dougherty and Alena Chekanov
Production Editorial: Sara Lerner
Jacket/Cover Design: Layla MacRory
Production: Erin Suydam
Publicity: Tayler Lord and Caroline Priday
Copyeditor: Sarah Vogelsong

This book has been composed in Adobe Text Pro and Gotham

Printed in the United States of America

Para mis tres madres

Norma, Tula, y Zoila

CONTENTS

ACKNOWLEDGMENTS

Shortly after getting my doctorate, I had a crisis of faith. I felt disconnected from academia, from philosophy, and, most disconcertingly, from my teaching. On a whim, I started reading Annette Lareau's *Unequal Childhoods*. That book opened up a new world for me. Suddenly, I saw my students, my own educational trajectory, and my ambivalence about academia in a new light. But philosophy, as Wittgenstein suggests, is a disease that, once caught, haunts the mind, and I was unable to read social science without asking myself philosophical questions about the nature of education and its role in shaping the world in which we live. Gradually, I found myself drawn to a field I hadn't even known existed—the philosophy of education. My ever-generous dissertation advisor Michael Bratman suggested that I chat with Debra Satz. And Debra, with her usual perspicacity, saw something interesting in my incoherent muddle of words. She encouraged me to apply for a grant from the Spencer Foundation. That organization's support, in particular that of Mike McPherson and Harry Brighouse, was crucial during the nascent stages of my thinking about education.

The real turning point in my interest in philosophy of education came when I arrived at the City College of New York. CCNY is a unique and special institution. My students are smart, funny, and generous, but more importantly, they are insightful in ways that are informed by their rich, complicated lives. They push me to be critical and reflective about what I teach and how I teach it. Without them, I would have never been able to write this book. CCNY, despite the significant financial limitations that it faces, has provided invaluable support for my research. I was very fortunate to receive a Professional Staff Congress—City University of New York Award, a City University of New York Scholar Incentive Award, a Book Completion Award, and a Gittell Junior Faculty Award—all of which were essential to the completion of this project. My colleagues in the Philosophy Department provided me with much-needed encouragement.

The philosophy of education community is a wonderfully warm and intellectually engaging group. I'm particularly grateful to Sigal Ben-Porath, Larry Blum, Eamonn Callan, Randal Curren, Jacob Fay, Tony Laden, Paula McAvoy, Michelle Moses, Rob Reich, Debra Satz, Gina Schouten, and Bryan Warnick for their support. Harry Brighouse has championed my work from the moment he read it. His encouragement and feedback have been invaluable to me. Meira Levinson convinced me that philosophy of education should not just espouse the ideas we care about, but maintain a dialogue with those who are affected by them. Her mentorship encouraged me to find a voice that transcended disciplinary boundaries.

I am eternally grateful for the support of Princeton University, which took a chance on me as an undergraduate and, again, by awarding me a Laurance S. Rockefeller Visiting Faculty Fellowship at the Center for Human Values for the 2015–2016 academic year. If this book is infused with the memories of my own undergraduate years, it is because I was fortunate to work on it while revisiting the sites of those experiences. There are so many people to thank for a wonderful year at the Center: Maureen Killeen and the rest of the staff for making sure that we had everything we needed to work, including kale salad and caffeine; the faculty at the Center that year—Charles Beitz, Johan Frick, Eric Gregory, Elizabeth Harman, Erika Kiss, Kim Lane, Melissa Lane, Stephen Macedo, Victoria McGreer, Phillip Petit, and Peter Singer—for ensuring that every event teemed with intellectual vibrance; and the other fellows—Chloe Bakalar, Luc Bovens, Marc Budolfson, Ruth Chang, Alexander Kirshner, Tal Lewis, Claudio Lopez-Guerra, Elinor Mason, Melinda Roberts, Geoffrey Sayre-McCord,

Monique Wonderly, and Nicholas Vrousalis—who made it a true intellectual wonderland. I was fortunate to start my dialogue about this book with Princeton University Press during that wonderful year. Ryan Mulligan helped me think through the early stages of this project, and Jessica Yao provided encouragement and feedback once the proposal was accepted. But this book wouldn't have made it to the finish line without the wise and patient advice of Peter Dougherty.

In order to complete this project, I had to "unlearn" my training in writing like a philosopher. David Lobenstine read many drafts of this manuscript and helped me articulate my ideas in a way that would allow me to reach nonphilosophers as well as philosophers. My research assistant and student Brandon Webley provided me with the essential student perspective on the project. Parts of this book were also written while I was on teaching leave thanks to a Philosophy and Science of Self-Control Grant from the Templeton Foundation and Florida State University, which I received in conjunction with my dear friend and extremely supportive collaborator Sarah Paul.

Many more people shared their stories with me than I was able to make a part of this book. I want to thank, with their permission, Emmania Blum, Emilie Lima Burke, James Cureton, Tammy Gewehr, Lissa Gregorio, Xiaoming Haugh, Simon Ives, T. J. Jefferson, Aja Kennedy, Katie LeBlanc, Jennifer Leon, Mickey Maki, Toni Moreno, Javiera Perez-Gomez, Juan Gabriel Ruiz, Joel Sati, Kavaris Sims, Waylon Smith, Joshua Spencer, Kimberly Tamayo, Krista Thomason, Doraine Toms, Rebecca Wellington, and Monique Wonderly, as well as others who chose to remain anonymous. Without their openness and generosity, I wouldn't have been able to complete this project. I am also deeply grateful to audiences at the City College of New York, Borough of Manhattan Community College, George Washington University, John Jay College, University of Texas–El Paso, Kansas State University, and the Philosophy, Politics, and Economics Program at the University of North Carolina–Chapel Hill for their feedback.

Finally, this book wouldn't have been written if it weren't for the support of my wonderful family. I am blessed with three mothers—Norma, Tulita, and Zoila—who each contributed in their own way to my education and continue to support me in my endeavors. I am also grateful for the support of my sister, Yamina, who understands the struggle of straddling worlds as an immigrant and a first-generation student. My husband, Jason, is not only a true co-parent and an excellent editor, but a bulwark against the tempest that writing a book brought to our home. He read every word in this book multiple times while working at a demanding architecture firm and caring for our energetic toddler. And I am so grateful for my daughter, Carolina, whose smile brightens every day. Finally, this book wouldn't have been possible if it weren't for my daughter's wonderful daycare teachers, in particular Ms. Miasia, Ms. Sophia, Ms. Narisara, and Ms. Julanna, who made sure she thrived while I worked on this manuscript. Our family is fortunate to be able to count on their support.

MOVING UP WITHOUT
LOSING YOUR WAY

Introduction

STRIVERS

Each of us starts off in a particular position in society. That position is determined by where and when you are born, the socioeconomic and educational level of your parents, your race, and your gender, among other things. Social scientists have produced vast amounts of evidence showing that these factors play a significant role in determining life prospects. In the United States, if you were born in the bottom fifth of the income scale in Charlotte, North Carolina, between 1980 and 1982, your chances of making it to the top fifth were 4.4 percent. If you had been born in San Jose, California, instead, your chances would have increased threefold.[1] Today, if you are born in the bottom tenth of the income scale and you are White, the probability that you will stay there is 17 percent. The probability goes up to 42 percent if you're Black.[2] If you are a woman born in the last 35 years, your chances of going to and completing college are higher than if you are a man. This is especially

1. Chetty et al., "Where Is the Land of Opportunity?"
2. Bowles, Gintis, and Osborne-Graves, *Unequal Chances*, 165.

true if you are a woman born to a wealthier family.[3] The data are dizzyingly complex. [4] What we know with a high degree of certainty is that if you were born in the United States within the past 20 years to a poor Black or Latino[5] family in an economically and racially segregated neighborhood, you are very likely to end up not far from where you started. Your children are likely to end up there too. The apple, as the saying goes, does not fall far from the tree.

The thought that your life opportunities will be determined by the accident of birth is diametrically opposed to the ideal of equal opportunity at the heart of the American Dream. As a society, we have viewed our educational institutions as *the* way of equalizing the prospects of those born into disadvantage. Optimists think education has the power to transform those prospects. They argue that we should focus on preparing more disadvantaged children to attend college because higher education has the power to propel them into the middle class. Pessimists think that schools can do very little to remedy the economic, social, and political injustices that exist more broadly across society and come to be reflected in it—segregated neighborhoods, lack of access to quality healthcare, racism, and poverty. They argue that many students born into disadvantage will never attend college, while those who do will face too many obstacles in their path. Optimists think that education has the power to transform lives; pessimists point out that this is the exception rather than the rule.

Education transformed my life prospects. I was born in a working-class neighborhood of Lima, Peru. The homes of secretaries and cab drivers shared the streets with factories emanating plumes of smoke. My grandmother had come to this neighborhood from Arequipa—a smaller city in the mountains of Peru. She

---

3. Bailey and Dynarski, "Inequality in Postsecondary Education."

4. The "bible" on this is Duncan and Murnane, *Whither Opportunity?*

5. Some prefer to use "Latinx" as a gender-neutral term to refer to those who have ancestral roots in Latin America. Though I am sympathetic to the rationale for using "Latinx," I have used the term "Latino," as most Latinos currently use this term to refer to their own community.

got pregnant young, married, quickly divorced, and raised two children while working full-time as a secretary at a movie theater. To my grandmother's disappointment, my mother got pregnant while she was still a teenager. While my mother found her footing, my grandmother, with the help of our extended family, raised me. Despite these challenges, our relative standing in Peruvian society was somewhere between working class and middle class. As my grandmother repeatedly points out, we never had to go hungry. Many Peruvians weren't so lucky. Nevertheless, the statistics would suggest that I was fated to repeat the story: I would barely finish high school, probably have a child young, and then work hard for the next 50 years just to make ends meet.

Luck intervened. My mother and aunt immigrated to Europe. There my aunt met and married a generous and wealthy man, and they helped pay for much of my education from that point on. Thanks to them, I was able to attend one of the most exclusive international schools in Peru from kindergarten through the twelfth grade. But Lima in the 1980s was economically depressed. Terrorism meant that our daily lives felt dangerous. My school was surrounded by armed guards, and cars were inspected for bombs as they entered. For as long as I can remember, my grandmother told me that to have a better and safer life I had to go abroad, though she didn't know exactly how this was going to happen. Fortunately, the college counselor at my school did. In my junior year, she called me into her office and explained to me that with my grades, I could get a good scholarship to attend university in the United States. So I joined the ranks of immigrants looking for a better life here. I became the first person in my family to graduate from college with a bachelor's degree, from Princeton, and then a doctorate, from Stanford. I am now a philosophy professor making a comfortable living in one of the richest countries in the developed world. I made it unusually far from the tree into which I was born.

I am well aware that my case is an anomaly. The social and economic structures within which we live often pose overwhelming challenges for students born into poverty. In order for more students from disadvantaged backgrounds to have a chance at succeeding in school and beyond, we must mitigate those challenges. But there are also lessons we can learn about the path of upward mobility from the anomalous cases of those who do manage to succeed. What I have learned, from my own life as well as from others who have gone through this experience, is that transcending the circumstances of one's birth comes with a heavy cost felt across many aspects of our lives that we value—relationships with family and friends, our connection to our communities, and our sense of identity. I call these the ethical costs of upward mobility. Understanding what these costs are, why they matter, and how to contend with them is the subject of this book.

Strivers

For most young people, the end of high school marks the beginning of a new phase in their lives. If you are one of the fortunate ones, college, with its promise of transformation and self-discovery, is just on the horizon. You might have heard funny and exciting stories from your parents, your friends' parents, or your neighbors about their own college experiences. You are probably looking forward to choosing your classes, joining social clubs, maybe becoming a member of a sorority or fraternity, and finding a major that suits your interests. Of course, you realize that you will have to work hard and be more independent than you have ever been—do your own laundry, feed yourself, and choose your classes. You might even be attending college thousands of miles away from home. You might be expected to work part-time to help pay for your living expenses, maybe by taking on a work-study job at the library. But all you have to worry about, your parents tell you, is taking advantage of this unique experience.

If you are a low-income or first-generation student, the end of high school also marks the beginning of a new phase in your life. College holds the promise of self-transformation, but also the possibility of transforming your life circumstances. You are, as I will call you, a striver. Your parents might not be entirely sure of what lies ahead, but they hope that you will be able to take advantage of opportunities that weren't available to them. They have not shared stories with you about their favorite professors, how they chose their major, or what it is like to attend Greek parties; you will have to figure out those aspects of college on your own. They expect you to get a college degree, but they might also expect you to help out at home, whether by working or by taking care of younger or sicker members of the family. You might have to take on large amounts of debt or work many hours to afford college. You probably have already been independent in many ways that are alien to your better-off classmates—you may have worked to contribute financially at home, taken care of siblings or relatives, or navigated many aspects of the college application process without parental help. Despite this, your parents might be nervous about you going off to college far away, preferring that you stay nearby. You've heard from family and friends that college is your ticket to a more comfortable life, but you have seen few people in your life succeed in that path. You are excited to go to college, but figuring out how to make it through and how to pay for it is daunting.

These sketches are highly schematic versions of two distinct experiences a student entering college might have. Many students fall somewhere in between these poles. Just as there is a variety of types of institutions of higher education that students attend—community colleges, technical schools, liberal arts colleges, public universities, and private universities—there is also a diversity of experiences among students pursuing postsecondary education. Some students who grow up in comfortable middle-class homes still struggle to afford college, working upward of 30 hours a week or taking on large amounts of debt to make ends meet.[6] Other working-class students are fortunate to end up at a university with a large endowment and find themselves enjoying privileges they

---

6. For a comprehensive, often-heartbreaking, look at the financial experiences of college students, see Goldrick-Rab, *Paying the Price*.

never imagined they would have. Dreamers, as they are known, go to college with the fear of being deported hanging over their heads, regardless of how well-off they are. My analysis focuses on the experiences of strivers because I believe that critically examining their case throws into sharp relief several crucial aspects of the experience of upward mobility that have been underappreciated.

I also focus on this group of students because a large part of the inspiration and motivation to write this book came from my experiences as a professor at the City College of New York (CCNY)—a large public university in the heart of Harlem—where many of my students are strivers. Townsend Harris, the founder of CCNY, declared that it was a place in which "the children of the rich and the poor take their seats together and know of no distinction save that of industry, good conduct, and intellect."[7] When it was founded, CCNY was free to attend and became known as the "Harvard of the Poor." It is no longer free, but the college has tried to stay true to its mission by retaining very low in-state tuition. CCNY is now part of the City University of New York (CUNY) system, which includes other four-year colleges, community colleges, and a graduate school with internationally renowned scholars and researchers. It serves over a quarter of a million students.[8] Of those, 78.2 percent are students of color, 38.5 percent come from families that make less than $20,000 a year, and 30 percent work more than 20 hours a week while in school. Additionally, 42 percent of our students are the first in their families to go to college. For many of these students, college is the path to the middle class.

CCNY students are a joy to teach. They bring insight and experiences into the classroom that consistently surprise me. Though there are certainly differences in academic preparation

7. City College of New York, "About Us."
8. City University of New York, "Profile of Undergraduates."

between my students and those I taught at my previous post at an elite liberal arts college, the most striking differences concern how much my students have to contend with outside of the classroom. Many of my students are negotiating extremely challenging conflicts between the demands of their families, friends, and community and those of their education. When my students are tired or absent, it isn't because they were out partying late, but because they needed to help take care of a sister, attend to a cousin in the hospital, or deal with emotionally charged and complicated dynamics at home. I've had students reveal to me that they are homeless, recovering from brain injuries, working 50-plus hours a week, and struggling to pay their mortgage. In a recent class I taught on the philosophy of race, we had a heated discussion about the differences in the disadvantages Americans face on the basis of race versus those on the basis of class. A bright young Latina told the class why she thought class mattered more than race—her mother had become disabled and was no longer able to work, so my student was now the principal breadwinner for her family, while attending college full-time. It's too much, she told us with tears in her eyes. Our ensuing discussion was incalculably enriched by her contribution, but it also revealed how challenging the path through college is for many of our students.

Strivers are born into families that face many of the challenges that working-class and poor families grapple with in this country. They are more likely to be unemployed or underemployed; to lack access to good healthcare, affordable childcare, and other benefits that professionals enjoy; and to live in neighborhoods with underresourced schools that serve other working-class and poor students. In the United States, disadvantage tends to be concentrated and segregated. In order to seek a better life for themselves, strivers must often enter different communities—those in which opportunities for advancement are available. As a result, a central aspect of the striver's experience is that of negotiating the distance between the community into which he or she was born and the one into which he or she seeks entry.[9]

The Ethical Costs of Striving

Most of us know that overcoming the circumstances of one's birth requires effort, time, and money. Working-class families make incredible sacrifices so that their children can access the opportunities that come from going to college and getting a degree. Much of the conversation about higher education focuses on college affordability, for good reason. The financial costs of college for strivers and even for many middle-class families these days are staggering.[10] Yet strivers face other costs along the path of upward mobility that are equally important, though rarely discussed. These costs are ethical; that is, they concern those aspects of a life that give it value and meaning—relationships with family and friends, connection to one's community, and one's sense of identity.

These ethical costs are the often-unacknowledged yet painful sacrifices that strivers must make as they journey along their path. Why are these costs ethical? Quite simply because they involve aspects of what, for most of us, count as essential elements of a good life. Family, friendship, and community—the aspects of a striver's life that we will consider—are vital to our flourishing as people. And this is why philosophers going back to Plato and Aristotle have been interested in these essential elements of our lives.[11]

Recognizing these costs as ethical allows us to understand why they are not easily accounted for in the way that financial or other

9. Princeton University Press's house style uses "he or she" when the gender of the subject is undefined. I do not mean for this choice to exclude nonbinary people who prefer to be referred to as "they." I realize that this is not an ideal solution and that some might feel excluded. However, I am committed to using "they" for persons who indicate such a preference.

10. Goldrick-Rab, *Paying the Price*.

11. For a wonderful contemporary reengagement with these questions, see Williams, *Ethics and the Limits of Philosophy*. For the classics, start with Plato, "Republic"; Aristotle, "Nichomachean Ethics."

costs are. Take, for example, student debt. It is certainly a stressful and common experience for students—strivers and, increasingly, those who are middle class—to accumulate debt while in college.[12] But we also know that students who do graduate college are more likely to be employed and to make more money than if they hadn't earned a degree. This debt is a long-term investment in their future. The short-term cost is offset by future gains. But, as we will see in chapter 1, the ethical costs strivers bear cannot be thought of in this way because they involve ethical goods that are not easily replaced. The weakening or loss of relationships with family and friends and ties to one's community are not easily compensated for by making new relationships or entering new communities.

Furthermore, those ethical costs are borne not only by strivers, but by their families and communities too. Initially I thought that many of my students at CCNY would do so much better academically if they went to a residential college away from home. Evidence supports this conjecture.[13] But I came to realize that this would come at a very serious cost. These students are sources of support, love, and inspiration to family, friends, and neighbors, and those relationships are sources of meaning and value in the lives of those whom they love. In turn, these experiences enrich my students' perspectives. The path upward for them is much more complicated than simply walking away.

Changing the Narrative

After completing my doctorate, I got a position as a visiting assistant professor at Swarthmore, an elite liberal arts college. My students there were fantastically well-read, intelligent, and academically well-prepared. I expected that. What I hadn't expected was how professional many of them already were. A few weeks into my

12. Goldrick-Rab, *Paying the Price.*
13. Bowen, Chingos, and McPherson, *Crossing the Finish Line.*

first semester, a very polite and smart young woman came into my office to tell me that the class dynamics weren't working for her. She was right—I had made the novice mistake of letting a few vocal students dominate the discussion. We talked about how I might go about changing those dynamics. What surprised me wasn't that this student had noticed that the class wasn't working—it was painfully obvious—but that she was able to come into my office and very calmly and clearly tell me what wasn't working. Some might scoff at her sense of "entitlement," but this would dismiss too easily what is actually a real set of professional skills that would serve this student quite well as she moved through college and, I have no doubt, into a successful career. She understood how to deal with authority figures and institutions, how to make sure her needs were heard, and how to advocate for herself. And she did all of this without ever seeming disrespectful. College was a place that she could navigate easily.[14]

Then I moved to New York to teach at City College. My students here are like those at Swarthmore in many respects, though they have a lot more to contend with outside of school. One key difference concerns the challenges they encounter in navigating their path to a degree. I have to try very hard to get my students to come talk to me during office hours. But those who need that interaction the most, those who are having trouble in class, will often simply disappear halfway through the semester. They get easily frustrated with themselves and view the challenges they confront as a negative reflection of their abilities, rather than as an expression of the difficulty of the topic, a failure on my part to explain it clearly, or a consequence of the difficult situations they contend with at home. It wouldn't occur to most of them to walk into my office and tell me that the class isn't working for them. As we will learn in chapter 2, these differences I have noticed in how students interact with me and with the institution, how they deal

---

14. For an excellent book on how well-off students are taught this kind of "ease," see Khan, *Privilege*.

with setbacks, how frequently they ask for help, how confident they are in their own opinions, and how comfortable they feel in the classroom environment are confirmed by what social scientists have found. This is not to say that my average CCNY student is deficient culturally or socially; rather, the point is that the culture and social world of college can be more difficult for them to navigate than it is for the privileged students at elite universities who have grown up preparing for this environment.

My efforts to better understand the challenges that my CCNY students face led me to the research that is the point of departure for this book. I was privileged as a college student in many ways that they are not, but nonetheless I identify with many of the ways in which they struggle. The first day I stepped off the airport shuttle at Princeton was also the first time I ever set foot on a college campus. My grandmother had cried at the airport while I tried to reassure her that everything would be fine, but neither of us had any idea what I was in for. On the shuttle, my anxiety started simmering as I overhead another first-year student chat away on her cell phone in at least three different languages with a confidence I could only aspire to have. Phillips Andover was mentioned several times. I didn't know then that it is one of the most exclusive boarding schools in the United States, if not the world. Feeling inadequate barely an hour into this new world, I lugged my embarrassingly large and heavy suitcase to the third floor of Blair Hall, shut the door, and wept on the bare mattress. It hit me for the first time that I was in a foreign country and that I would have to figure it out all by myself.

But I had another advantage that I have noticed many strivers lack—I had a narrative that allowed me to conceptualize my experience in a helpful way. Even though my family could not offer me guidance about the transition to college, they had prepared me for being an immigrant, and that framing, it turned out, was incredibly useful. Everybody in my immediate family had emigrated for economic opportunities—my great-grandfather from a canyon in the depths of the Andes to the closest regional city; my grandmother from that city to Lima, the capital; and my mother and my aunt from Peru to Europe. I was taught that to access opportunities for upward mobility I would have to eventually move far from home and that it would be hard and lonely work. This way of understanding my experience prepared me to confront some of the toughest challenges I faced. Crucially, unlike the narrative of upward mobility students are often offered, the narrative I was offered was much more honest about the ethical costs I would face.

The traditional narrative of upward mobility in this country acknowledges the academic and financial hurdles that strivers have to overcome to succeed, but it does not do a good job of preparing students for the emotional, psychological, and ethical challenges they will confront. We rarely tell students that their success may come at the expense of some of the things that they hold most dear—their relationships with family and friends, their connection to their communities, and their sense of who they are and what matters to them. Many of us who play a role in the education of strivers operate with a very narrow and reductive view of the challenges they face. I believe that we need to reconceive this narrative to be more honest with students about the challenges they will confront in these other important areas of their life.

In this book I outline the elements of a new narrative of upward mobility, one that is honest about the ethical costs involved. Each of the first four chapters addresses one particular element of this narrative. The first involves recognizing the ethical costs of upward mobility as distinct. Chapter 1 describes these costs and presents an argument for why they are different from other costs that strivers face on their path. The second element of the ethical narrative involves situating those ethical costs in their appropriate context. Chapter 2 argues that these ethical costs are unfairly leveled on students born into disadvantage for three contingent reasons: socioeconomic segregation, an inadequate safety net, and cultural mismatch. This chapter shows us that many of the ethical costs strivers face are not a necessary feature of striving itself but are instead dependent on how opportunities are unequally distributed in the United States. The third element of the ethical narrative involves navigating one's evolving identity. Chapter 3 focuses on the idea of codeswitching—changing how one behaves as one moves between the community one is attempting to join and the one in which one's family and friends reside—in order to avoid incurring ethical costs and retain a sense of one's identity. I argue that this is an ethically fraught exercise that must be done with care. Strivers need to be reflective about what they value in order to avoid compromising in ways that they will come to regret. The fourth element of the ethical narrative, explored in chapter 4, is the need for strivers to think about their potential complicity within the social structures that make it hard for others who are disadvantaged to succeed. I argue that strivers are in a unique position to improve those structures because of the skills and knowledge they acquire on the path upward. Chapter 5 weaves these elements together to present an ethical narrative of upward mobility that is more honest about the true nature of the costs of moving up and the responsibility we all bear for those costs.

Methodology

This book is a work of ethics insofar as it contends with topics that concern the valuable and meaningful aspects of a human life, but in writing it I also hope to illuminate important aspects of the experience of upward mobility in a way that will speak to those who are striving—first-generation and low-income college students—and those of us who are concerned with enabling these strivers to succeed—professors, administrators, and policymakers. My hope is that this book will move us to embrace a new narrative of upward mobility through education, one that is honest about the true costs as well as the benefits of this enterprise.[15]

---

15. My approach has been inspired by Meira Levinson's approach to philosophy of education, which takes as its point of departure the actual lived experiences of teachers and students rather than abstract philosophical theorizing. See, in particular, her *No Citizen Left Behind.*

A central idea driving this book is that narratives are powerful tools in shaping our understanding of ourselves and our future. It is important, then, that the ideas in this book are not only backed up by arguments or evidence from the social sciences, though I provide both, but also illustrated by the stories of real-life strivers. I interviewed 28 strivers—some in person, others through Skype or e-mail, and still others by phone. I approached these conversations as a philosopher interested in the perspectives of those who had experienced the profound transformative effect of education on their life prospects. I wanted to know how they looked back on the sacrifices they had made in order to succeed. But these interviews were not intended to serve as a rigorous, systematic empirical study of the experiences of first-generation students. Rather, they are meant to show us that narratives of upward mobility are far more ethically complicated than is generally acknowledged.

So many of those who got in touch with me told me that they did so because they felt that this project was important. Many of them wished that they had had a book that would have helped them make sense of their experiences. I have given all the participants pseudonyms—the asterisk accompanying a newly introduced name indicates this—and I have tried my best to keep their words as they wrote or said them. I learned so much from their stories, and their words have made this book incalculably richer. To them I am eternally grateful.

I refer to my own experience throughout because this was my entry point into the topic of this book. I am a person of color, a first-generation college graduate, and an immigrant. However, my experience is not typical of the striver's path in many ways. As someone who has been educated in elite institutions all of my life, whose family has become much wealthier since I was born, and who has largely adapted and assimilated to the educated, American upper-middle class, I am not claiming that my own journey is representative of the experiences of most students of color, immigrants, or those born into poverty. I infuse my story into this book because I think it is important that in a work concerning the ways in which our backgrounds and educational experiences shape us, the voice and experiences of the author are clearly revealed. But I do so also because this book originated from an empathetic impulse—as I tried to understand my students, I saw some of the challenges I confronted magnified in their experiences. I wanted that connection to remain a part of the text.

Finally, I include stories drawn from my experience teaching strivers. I do so for two reasons. The first is that I want to show how the ethical costs discussed in this book play out in the interactions students and professors have in the classroom. I hope that these vignettes will help other educators reading this book to draw connections to their own classrooms. The second is that much of what I have learned about strivers I have learned from my students. They are the motivation and inspiration for this book. Without them, the ideas in this book would have been impoverished.

The way we typically conceive, or misconceive, of the path of upward mobility does a disservice to strivers. As I will argue in this book, the traditional narrative of upward mobility obscures the true costs that they will face and consequently is fundamentally dishonest. But the central argument of this book also has deep political implications. Inequality in the United States is not only growing, but becoming increasingly entrenched in families and communities. Education is one tool to mitigate that intergenerational entrenchment. Through education, children can be given the knowledge and skills to ascend into a better socioeconomic position than that of their parents. Those who succeed might be able to help their families and serve as role models for others in their community. This is the promise of education for upward mobility, but it ignores the true costs of this model to low-income communities.

For those born into families and communities that are heavily disadvantaged, moving up the socioeconomic ladder often involves moving away. This is especially true if strivers want to provide their own children with access to better schools and safer neighborhoods than they grew up with. But this impulse, while understandable, undermines vital resources disadvantaged communities need to create opportunities for advancement from within. When those who gain the social, economic, and cultural knowledge to improve their socioeconomic standing move away from disadvantaged communities, valuable human capital walks away with them. This phenomenon is often called "brain drain," but the deleterious effect on the fabric of social relationships within the community is more than economic. What is drained out of the community is also a son, a sister, a cousin, a neighbor, a babysitter, a mentor. These bonds within the community have the potential to enrich the lives of those who live in it, and when upward mobility is in tension with these bonds, the community suffers. In this book, I argue that we need a new narrative of upward mobility. But what I hope to have convinced you of by the time you reach the conclusion is that what we need is a new model of upward mobility, one that lifts communities and not just individuals.

1

Recognizing the Ethical Costs of Upward Mobility

Sandra* rushes into my office 15 minutes late for our appointment. Her hair is wet from the rain. She starts apologizing profusely before she even sets her bag down. I smile and try to reassure her that I'm not upset; I know that the 1 train is notoriously dreadful on a day like this. Sandra is nervous, and she has good reason to be. Her tardiness and absences are starting to become a serious problem. When she does come to class, though she tries hard to keep up with the conversation, she can barely keep her eyes open. She hasn't turned in a few of the weekly reading responses, and the due date for a major paper is fast approaching.

At first, she tries to convince me that I should accept her reading responses several weeks late. She tells me that she really meant to turn them in, but she was running late, and the train, and work . . . Her voice trails off. I have a reputation for being strict about deadlines. Sandra knows there is little she can do to convince me. I'm sympathetic but explain the rationale for my policy clearly and firmly. She might not recognize it, but this is probably for the best. I can already see that if she were to try and "catch up'" by making up missed work, her prospects in the class would be even worse. Each individual reading response does not make up much of her final grade, but the grade she receives on the upcoming paper matters. That is what she needs to concentrate on.

As we talk, a larger story emerges. Sandra tells me that she's been dealing with a lot of "family drama" back home. This is a catchall phrase for the situations many of my students confront: sick siblings or children, parents who need help with childcare or chores, relatives who are in legal or financial trouble. I listen sympathetically, but I don't ask for more details. My focus as Sandra's professor is on making sure she does well in class. I need to encourage her to turn her attention to the upcoming assignment. My pedagogical goal is to have her walk out of my office with a mental outline that breaks up the task of writing the paper into smaller, less daunting steps. I know from the first few weeks of class that she is a smart student and a strong writer; now I must convince her that her skills are up to the challenge of this assignment, regardless of what else is happening in her life.

Lurking beneath this exchange is a larger, more difficult conversation about how to confront conflicts between her education and those other important, yet competing, concerns. Finishing college, my colleagues and I regularly tell students like Sandra, is of crucial importance. If Sandra drops out, she is much more likely to be unemployed. Even if she finds a job, the odds are that she will make significantly less money than she would have if she had completed her degree.[1] If she accumulates debt while attending college, as many students do, she may end up worse off economically than when she started. But though she might understand this in the abstract, what is more difficult to contend with is the reality that to successfully complete her degree, she will often have to prioritize her education over her family, friends, and community. Sandra is doing everything she can to fulfill all of those obligations, but I can see that it is too much. The stress is visible in the

1. Bureau of Labor Statistics, *Unemployment Rates and Earnings.*

way her shoulders slump and in how her voice breaks during tense moments in our conversation. If she is to succeed in college, she will have to learn to say no to those for whom she cares. This will involve making difficult sacrifices in areas of her life that she finds valuable and meaningful, perhaps even central to her sense of who she is. And it is this difficult conversation that faculty and administrators so often skirt around when addressing the barriers to graduation that students like mine face.

Many disadvantaged students frequently confront the sort of situation that Sandra finds herself facing. Their path toward upward mobility is beset with conflicts and sacrifices. It might seem obvious that, as her professor, I should advise her to prioritize her education over those competing concerns. Though such advice is well meaning, it often disregards the painful reality of carrying it out. What would it take for Sandra to really follow that advice? What sacrifices would she have to make in order to graduate? How will her relationships with her family change when she starts placing a higher priority on finishing her degree? It is crucial that those who want to support students on this path—teachers, professors, mentors, families—fully appreciate what they are asking students to do. And, as I will suggest throughout this book, it is extremely important that strivers—those disadvantaged students who are on the path of upward mobility—recognize the nature of the sacrifices they will have to make.

It is widely accepted that strivers must make difficult sacrifices to transcend the circumstances into which they are born. What hasn't been adequately appreciated is that some of the most important sacrifices strivers make are *ethical*, that is, they concern the most meaningful and valuable aspects of a good life. What is potentially on the line is not just money, time, or hard work, but their relationships with friends and family, the bonds they have with their community, and sometimes even their sense of identity. In order to distinguish the ethical sacrifices strivers make from other costs discussed by economists and social scientists, let's call these goods *ethical goods* and the sacrifice of them *ethical costs*.

The central idea of this book is that just as we take into account other costs of going to college for strivers—money, time, effort—we should consider the ethical costs as well. We turn to ethics in order to understand these costs because it is the study of precisely that which makes life good and valuable. In this chapter, I argue that understanding the nature of these ethical goods moves us well beyond the cost-benefit analysis that might be appropriate when thinking about money, time, or effort. The ethical costs of upward mobility are particular and not easily offset. Consequently, their loss is felt keenly by those who succeed even if they ultimately have much to gain from the sacrifices they have made.

This book is aimed both at those who want to support strivers in their path through college and at strivers themselves. Those who are concerned with the challenges faced by first-generation and low-income college students often fail to appreciate the significance of the potential ethical costs that strivers encounter in pursuing a better life for themselves. And though strivers know these sacrifices intimately, I hope that a thorough discussion of their nature can allow them to articulate more clearly the challenges they face.

Todd's and Henry's Stories of Upward Mobility

Many of those I interviewed for this book shared inspiring stories of upward mobility. I heard from professionals whose lives are dramatically different than those of their parents or the friends with whom they grew up. They have college degrees. They own their homes. They thrive professionally. Not only are they financially better off than their own families were when they were growing up, but their lives are rich and full of those ethical goods that are important and meaningful—partners, friends, work they enjoy. And they got there through education and hard work. Todd* and Henry* are no exception.

Todd, a bright and affable African American man, grew up in a predominantly minority neighborhood in Atlanta with his grandparents, mother, and sister. As Todd described it, the neighborhood had experienced extreme decline in the 1970s, and when he was growing up it was "not the best neighborhood, a lot of crime, a few projects nearby." Todd's mother had been a drug addict. She had irregular employment with long stretches of unemployment. His dad was mostly out of the picture. Todd went to the local public school, which was, as he described it, "100 percent Black" and notoriously "crappy." Since much of his extended family lived in the area, his cousins as well as his sister went to the same school.

Todd disliked the neighborhood school. He was teased by other students for "trying to be White," which he interpreted as a reference to studying and getting good grades.[2] After a teacher was stabbed at the school, his mother asked a friend of hers to let them use her address so that Todd would be eligible to attend a predominantly White, middle-class, suburban magnet school. As Todd pointed out with a hint of embarrassment in his voice, this was "technically not above board, but you know . . ." Because his mother couldn't drive him to school, Todd drove himself, despite not being a fully licensed driver. Again, this strategy was not legal, but, as he saw it, it was necessary to gain those educational opportunities unavailable in his neighborhood. Without guidance from his family, Todd managed to navigate the college application process and found a way to become the first person in his family to go to college. When I met him, he was pursuing a master's degree at an Ivy League university after a few years working in the federal

2. This comment by Todd touches on a highly contentious topic of debate among social scientists—whether there is a culture of poverty that can be blamed for the educational underachievement of some minority groups. In a seminal paper, Signithia Fordham and John U. Ogbu argued that African American students often adopt a culture that is in opposition to mainstream White culture, and that in this "oppositional culture" doing well in school is not valued (see their "Black Students' School Success"). Much of the subsequent research has put this theory in doubt. For more on this debate, see Ainsworth-Darnell and Downey, "Assessing the Oppositional Culture Explanation"; Tyson, Darity, and Castellino, "It's Not 'a Black Thing.'" I discuss some of this work in the following chapter.

government. His prospects were bright. He is now happily married to a similarly well-educated woman and is pursuing a career in the foreign service.

Henry, now a successful White academic, grew up in the Pacific Northwest with his mother, brother, and sister in a working-class neighborhood. His mother and grandmother had grown up in extreme poverty, and Henry's own childhood was also marred by poverty. His mother worked off and on at low-paying part-time jobs to support the family. His father didn't play a significant role in his upbringing. The family lived in Section 8 housing—government-subsidized housing for low-income families—and received food vouchers, welfare, and free school lunches. Heat and hot water were scarce, as they are for many poor families. In the winter, the whole family relied on one space heater, which they called "the God." Sometimes they had to heat hot water on the stove to bathe. They didn't have a phone at home and for a year had to do without a refrigerator because the landlord refused to fix it. Henry described his memories of growing up as "feeling isolated and lonely . . . partly [as] a result of our socioeconomic situation, particularly, our lack of phone, my embarrassment over our living situation, and the fact that I couldn't afford to do normal things like go to the movies with friends."

Henry's mother had a high regard for education. Throughout Henry's childhood she slowly took the courses she needed to get a college degree, eventually earning an associate's degree. Like Todd, Henry didn't receive much guidance at home about how to apply for a four-year college, so he enrolled in the local community college that his mother attended. Eventually, he transferred to a four-year college away from home because he "worried that various problems at home would compel [him] to slow down [his] education or even drop out." This was quite clear-sighted of Henry. I have seen how hard it is for many of my students to live at home and not allow what is happening there to negatively impact their college trajectory. Henry flourished in college, went on to a graduate program in philosophy, and is now an associate professor at a well-respected public university. He is happily married. He and his wife both have good incomes and own their home.

Todd and Henry, through hard work and education, managed to overcome their circumstances. Statistics tell us that these cases are anomalous. Todd's mother and grandparents didn't go to college, yet he managed to not only enroll in college but graduate and thrive afterwards. After he received his bachelor's degree, the opportunities available to him far surpassed those that would be expected to be within reach of someone growing up in his neighborhood. Once he receives his master's degree from an Ivy League university, his prospects will be even brighter than he could have imagined as a young boy. Henry also grew up in poverty, but still he managed not only to finish college, but to earn a Ph.D. and become a well-respected tenured professor.

These stories awe and inspire us. They also conform to a well-rehearsed narrative of upward mobility in which the sacrifice of time, money, and effort earns one a myriad of rewards later on. Todd worked throughout college and wasn't able to partake in many social opportunities because of it. Henry lived very frugally on his student loans and saved enough money to start paying them off as soon as he graduated. These sacrifices are what we imagine it takes for a striver to succeed. What the narrative obscures is the ethical costs that are also a part of the ledger.

Understanding Ethical Goods

One of the ways in which we give shape to our lives is by investing our time and effort into activities, goals, and relationships we find valuable. Those projects and relationships end up giving a life its distinctive contours. Take a moment to ask yourself what you value in your life. Many of us will respond to this question by citing family, friends, community, projects or interests, and, if we are lucky, work. These are the aspects of life that I have suggested we call *ethical goods*. They are distinct from those other aspects of our life that are important—financial security, material goods, and time—but that generally matter to us because they enable our engagement with the ethical goods that are most meaningful to us.[3]

Ethical goods matter to us in and of themselves, but they also matter to our sense of identity. Most of us think of our identities as closely tied to those ethical goods in which we are invested. My relationship with my daughter is crucial to my identity as a mother. My engagement with my students is a part of what constitutes my identity as a teacher. My relationship, or lack thereof, with a Peruvian community informs my sense of myself as Peruvian. What this means is that a loss or weakening of those relationships is not only a loss of something that matters to me but a threat to my sense of identity.

Children and young people haven't yet determined many of the ethical goods that will engage them and become a part of their future identities. For them, the future is open, full of possibility. As they become invested in certain activities, goals, and relationships, their life starts to take on its distinctive character and value.[4] But this should not lead us to overlook how much of young people's lives is valuable and meaningful to them *now*.[5] Relationships with family, friends, peers, teachers, and others in the community form the backbone of their developing sense of identity.[6] Of course, there are many other aspects of young people's lives that are valuable and meaningful to them for the future promise they hold—education, the discovery and development of their talents, a variety of projects and interests—but what is often at stake for strivers is precisely those ethical goods that are so central to their development and their self-conception now.

---

3. We can also make this point by saying that time, money, and material goods matter instrumentally, whereas the ethical goods in question matter intrinsically.

4. For a thoughtful philosophical discussion of what we owe children whose future is open in this way, see Feinberg, "Child's Right to an Open Future."

5. Robert Noggle develops a careful philosophical position that aims to respect a child's burgeoning values. See his "Special Agents."

6. For an overview of the importance of those early caregivers as understood by attachment theory, see Bretherton, "Origins of Attachment Theory."

I don't intend to offer a general analysis of ethical goods here. That is the task of a lifetime. Rather, I'm going to focus on the sort of ethical goods that are so often at stake for strivers—relationships with family, friends, and community. In order to understand why sacrificing these goods is so consequential to a striver's life, we need to reflect on two important characteristics they possess. The first is that these goods are particular, and the second is that they are not easily replaced.

PARTICULARITY

The fact that I spend my time chatting with my husband after a long day at work, playing with my toddler, cultivating close friendships, using my vacation to visit my grandmother in Peru, worrying about my book, and attending to my students' progress says something fundamental about who I am and what I find valuable. It is tempting to describe these values using general categories: marriage, parenting, friendship, family, research, and teaching. But I don't value marriage as a general category; rather, I value my specific relationship with my actual husband. If my husband were replaced with another equally intelligent and funny man in the middle of the night, I would be understandably upset![7]

This is a fanciful philosopher's example, but it points to an important aspect of how we relate to many aspects of our life that give it value and meaning—they are *particular*. It is *this* friend, *this* child, *this* community, and *this* career that matter to us. Much of our lives is devoted to advancing the wellbeing and flourishing of particular people and projects. My daughter Carolina, my husband Jason, my friend Sarah, the people who make up my community in New York, and my career as a philosopher fill out the contours of a life devoted to parenting, marriage, friends, community, and

---

7. In the philosophical literature on love, philosophers argue that what we love and value is particular. See Frankfurt, *Reasons of Love*; Jollimore, *Love's Vision*; Scheffler, "Valuing."

meaningful work. This point is important in helping us better understand the significance of what is at stake for strivers. The loss of ethical goods that are particular in this way is unlike other kinds of loss.

NOT EASILY REPLACED

The fact that the ethical goods in question are particular means that when those aspects of our life fade or wane, their loss is not canceled out by gaining something else of value. When we lose people, communities, and relationships that matter to us, they are not easily replaced. Consider losing a dear friend to an illness. Even if you then go on to make another friend as a result of that experience—for example, in a survivor support group—the void left in your life by the first friend's passing isn't simply erased by the gain of the second friend. The resulting pain might be mitigated by the joys of making a new friend, but what you valued was that particular person in your life, and she can't simply be replaced by a new person.[8] In this respect, the ethical goods in question are different than other resources one might lose, such as money or material goods, which are, in general, replaceable.[9]

Of course, not all relationships are special or meaningful to us. Some relationships might be easily replaced without much loss. After a move, the role a pleasant neighborly acquaintance plays in our lives might be filled by an equally pleasant new neighbor. But when a person or project or community matters to us deeply, we value it in its particularity, and it is not easily replaced by another. The loss in such cases is experienced as meaningful even if there is much to be gained from it.

With these two ideas in hand, we can start to see why the standard way of portraying upward mobility falls short. According

---

8. I discuss the idea of mitigating ethical goods in the final chapter.

9. For a philosophical discussion of the link between value and irreplaceability, see Cohen, "Rescuing Conservatism."

to the story many of us have grown up hearing, being a striver involves sacrificing time, financial resources, and effort, but those short-term losses are made up for by substantial long-term gains. The investment of $15,000 in tuition now can be made up for by the large gains in income one will get with a college degree in hand later. Families and communities might also benefit from strivers' success. Some strivers might be inclined to help their families financially or to invest in their communities once they are able to do so. Furthermore, the gains that result from an education are not merely economic, but improvements to one's life in a deeper sense. Going to college can be transformative. Students gain knowledge about the world around them and their place in it. They may develop a taste for literature, music, and other art forms that they might not have been exposed to otherwise. In interacting with other students and faculty, they become better thinkers and communicators. As philosopher John Stuart Mill suggests, a university education should aim to make one a "capable and cultivated human being," not simply prepare one for being a lawyer or doctor.[10] Communities may gain as well from having strivers succeed and go on to serve as role models for other young people. This narrative portrays the path of upward mobility as the accumulation of net gains. However, even though when we balance the losses and gains, most strivers end up having gained considerably from their success—not just financially, but in many valuable areas of their life—that doesn't mean that the losses incurred are made whole.

By working hard, Todd and Henry gained educational and career opportunities that would have been unimaginable to many who grew up like they did. In the process, they were exposed to ideas, people, and ways of life that they might not have experienced had they stayed at home. There is undeniable value in all of this. Neither expressed regret for their choices, and both acknowledged how much better off they were compared to others who had started out like they did. But to assume that those gains

---

10. Mill, "Inaugural Address," 186.

simply balanced out the losses experienced in the process fails to acknowledge the value of the goods that the two men sacrificed.

Todd's and Henry's Stories Revisited

Todd grew up in a neighborhood that despite its disadvantages was woven deeply into his family's life. His extended family—cousins, aunts, and uncles—had gone to the same neighborhood school and would drop by his grandparents' house regularly. He told me that his "family was kind of weird in the sense that first cousins, second cousins, third cousins, all live in the same areas. We're all there. So, there's like 80 to 90 people at any given time who are cousins." Todd's social circle began to change when he switched to the magnet school. There he started hanging out with kids who were mostly White and whose parents were white-collar professionals like dentists and doctors.

Even as Todd grew comfortable in his new social circle, he couldn't completely relax. He was worried about someone discovering that he wasn't attending the school legally. He kept his life at home largely hidden from his new friends. He had a few girlfriends whose parents welcomed him into their home, but, as he told me, "I would always avoid conversations with them, where I came from, where I actually live, because I thought it was too stark of a difference. I thought that would be a reason for them to say, 'Oh, my daughter can't see you anymore.'"

His new friends took it for granted that they were going to college, unlike the kids in his neighborhood. Todd learned what he could from them and applied to college himself. When he arrived at college he experienced what he described as "a culture shock." He was well prepared academically, but socially he experienced a persistent "feeling of still being other." Some of the struggles were financial; he found it hard to find the time or money to participate in the social activities in which his peers were involved. But the disconnect went deeper. He told me, "I felt okay walking around campus. . . . I could blend in a little. But once I said or did something to break the illusion, I felt that it would all fall apart." These feelings continued in Todd's prestigious internship and, later, his government job. He said: "I didn't really get close to anyone. I didn't really make any friends . . . I think partially because we came from different backgrounds. It was hard for me." At various points, Todd was part of many different communities—his childhood neighborhood, high school, college, and workplace. Yet even as he became more a part of the communities of those who shared his level of education, he felt it difficult to connect with others in a way that would allow him to forge those new relationships.

At the same time, his relationship with his family was weakening. At first, while he was in college, he would visit home often. But as he moved farther away, he "completely cut off from them because I just wasn't running in the same circles as they were and not doing the same things that they were." When Todd moved to the Northeast, the expense of driving home became an additional deterrent. But there was another factor that also contributed to straining his connection to his family. As he told me, "A lot of my relationship with them had become very monetized in a way. . . . Whenever they called me, it was always about money." Todd sent his family money as soon as he started working, but his sister never thought it was enough. His calls became more infrequent because it was difficult to say no to his family's requests.

This situation was not easy for Todd. Though there was much he had gained by taking advantage of the educational and career opportunities in front of him, a deep sense of loss pervaded our conversation. When I asked him to reflect on what he would tell his younger self, he expressed some regret about the trade-offs he had made. He told me: "It was almost like I was given the choice . . . to sacrifice relationships for being able to survive college. I would tell my past self to try to find ways not to do that, try to find ways to not make it such a trade-off. To maybe find ways to make it more involved, like, you can still have your family there and you can still reach out to them and be with them, and not have this fear of falling back into their ways."

Todd was clearly proud of everything he had achieved. Yet he felt conflicted about what he had had to give up in the process. His connection to his family and community became increasingly tenuous the more he achieved. And though he slowly gained new friendships, new relationships, and a new community, these gains did not simply cancel out the connections he had lost.

Henry's trajectory echoes Todd's in many respects. Henry recalled that "the hardest part about college [was] feeling . . . culturally out of place and my worries and guilt about my family." His sister, who at the time was struggling with drug addiction, asked to live with him during his second year at college. Henry wrote: "She asked if she could live in [college] with me and I said yes. I neither believed nor disbelieved that my sister would be able to kick her drug habit. But I wanted to give her the chance to move out of the environment [back home] and I wanted to give my mom some relief." The arrangement didn't last long, and his sister continued to struggle with her addiction afterward.

Henry grew more and more depressed and sought counseling. But when one of his counselors suggested he had no responsibilities toward his family, he grew angry. Walking away from them wasn't easy or uncomplicated, even if he felt that it was often necessary to achieve the goals he had set for himself. As he saw it:

> I do not think I could have helped to prevent any of the various things that happened to my family from happening. I doubt the overall trajectory of their lives would have been much different had I stayed. . . . My sister would still have struggled with addiction, my mom would still have been kicked out of her house, and all the various other events that I have not mentioned probably would have occurred too. But I would have been there for them. I would have been there, helpful and caring, with my family.

Yet again, Henry's analysis is astute—there was little he could have done to solve all of his family's problems. But he was also right that by being there, he would have been able to show his family that he cared and to share in their pain. His distance frayed those relationships, though maintaining that distance probably was the only way he could have succeeded on his path. Reflecting on his experience, he wrote: "When I think about them I feel like I have no soul. I keep walking away." The keen sense of loss Henry experienced wasn't assuaged by everything he had gained. He also thought his choices reflected something about himself he found troubling.

Once we dig deeper into Todd's and Henry's stories, we begin to see the ways in which the relationships that are valuable to most of us—those with family, friends, and our communities—are particularly vulnerable to fraying on the path of upward mobility. A central difficulty for both men involved seeking a balance between maintaining the ethical goods that shaped their early lives and seeking opportunities for advancement. To find a path upward, strivers must often enter new communities, with their own distinct sets of demands. But those communities are distant, literally and metaphorically, from the families, friends, and home communities of these strivers. In becoming a part of those communities, they risk their engagement with ethical goods closer to home. It is these trade-offs and sacrifices that are largely invisible in the uplifting narratives of upward mobility we are used to hearing.

I would like to draw our attention to two points that emerge as we read through these stories. First, the ethical costs involved in upward mobility give rise to complicated feelings, sometimes even regret and guilt.[11] It might be tempting to dismiss these feelings as irrational, as Henry's therapist did, but I urge us to hold off on making that judgment. The appropriate response to the loss of something we value is to feel regret. And it is not unreasonable to feel guilt when your own choices play a role in that loss. Even when a striver is sure that his or her choices are the right ones, feelings of moral ambiguity may remain. That ambiguity often reflects

11. For a heartbreaking discussion of these feelings from the perspective of a counselor and psychologist, see Jensen, *Reading Classes*.

something deeply important about what is at stake—and recognizing that importance doesn't require us to change our evaluation that the striver did the right thing.

Second, the ethical costs of upward mobility are borne not just by the striver, but by his family, friends, and community. When a valuable relationship is lost or weakened, both parties lose something valuable. When a striver's relationship with his or her family deteriorates, the family suffers as well. When a friendship is lost, two people lose a friend. When a striver's connection to his or her community is severed, the community also bears the loss of a motivated and talented member. Ethical costs are also borne by those who stay behind. We will return to this very important point in the chapters that follow.

Trading Off Ethical Goods

Only 21 percent of low-income, first-generation students who enroll in higher education will receive a degree compared with 57 percent of students who are not low-income or first-generation.[12] Many of these first-generation students hope to achieve upward mobility by attending college, but their paths get disrupted. No doubt many of those disruptions are the result of financial, academic, and other hardships that low-income students face, but an honest account of the hurdles faced by such students should include the potential ethical costs students are liable to pay.[13] I do not mean to suggest that these costs fully or largely explain the lack of completion rates among this student population. However, in order to understand the full spectrum of costs

12. One of the biggest challenges in higher education is that of college completion, in particular among low-income students. See Bowen and McPherson, *Lesson Plan*; Cahalan et al., "Indicators of Higher Education Equity."

13. We should not overlook the role of food and housing insecurity in college completion and success. For more on this issue, see Goldrick-Rab, *Paying the Price*.

that strivers face, we shouldn't overlook the ethically meaningful portion of the ledger.[14]

Understanding these costs matters not only because doing so might help us better understand why strivers' paths get disrupted, but also because these costs are different in important ways from other kinds of costs. As we have noted, what is often at stake for strivers—relationships with family and friends, ties to their community, and sense of identity—are ethical goods that are particular, not easily replaced, and important to the lives most of us hope to lead. Consequently, their loss is a particularly difficult cost to bear, one that is not easily mitigated, even by the many gains that are reaped from educational and career success. In this section, we will investigate how these goods are traded off. With this analysis in hand, we will be able to understand the argument, developed fully in the following chapter, that strivers are more likely to bear these costs in a society, like our own, that suffers from socioeconomic segregation, an inadequate safety net, and cultural forces that privilege those who are already otherwise advantaged.

PRIORITIZING ETHICAL GOODS UNDER CONSTRAINTS

In valuing my relationship with a family member or friend, I have a reason to devote myself to it that I wouldn't have otherwise.[15] I spend time and energy thinking about how to help my friend Sarah when she needs emotional support because she is an important part of my life. If I did not value our friendship, then she would not play the same role in my thinking and action that she does now. This is another way of saying that valuing a good, whether it is a friendship or a family relationship, requires that we *prioritize* it

14. No doubt more social science research has to be conducted to understand how and when these kinds of costs arise. My role as a philosopher is to explain the nature of these goods in order to understand how their loss affects the ethical life of those who must bear them.

15. For a sophisticated philosophical discussion of this idea, see Scheffler, *Boundaries and Allegiances*.

when making decisions. But we are also finite beings with limited time and resources—we cannot prioritize everything. As a consequence, we face *ethical conflicts*—situations in which two or more goods we value are at play and we cannot prioritize them both. In such cases, we must decide to put our time and effort into one thing we value at the expense of another. That is, we must make a *trade-off*—a sacrifice in one valuable domain of our lives for the sake of a gain in another.

Trade-offs arise because we are constrained by how much time, money, or attention we can invest in a particular good. These constraints are not inherently a bad thing. Friendship is a special relationship in part because we cannot have that kind of relationship with everyone. We only choose some people to make a part of our lives in this way. Constraints allow us to focus our energy on a few goods, whether they be people, projects, or goals, and these become important to who we are and what we value. Sometimes the conflicts we face are easy to resolve. I will choose to spend time with my daughter over many other projects and goods that I value because I do not value them nearly as much as my relationship with her.

But even though we all face constraints, the constraints we face are not all equal. For those in poverty, the constraints imposed by not having enough time, money, or attention to devote to the goods in their lives are acute and can have a negative effect on their ability to lead flourishing lives. Furthermore, when other areas of one's life are already severely restricted by a lack of resources and opportunities, any potential harm to one's relationships with family, friends, or community is especially disheartening.

Think back to Sandra, who we saw struggling to balance all of her obligations at the beginning of this chapter. The particular details of the real Sandra's situation are no doubt complex; for the sake of our discussion, I will rely on a composite, fictionalized picture of Sandra based on my experiences teaching students like her. Suppose that Sandra's sister is sick and needs caretaking. Now she has to decide between attending to her sister or attending an important class. She is facing an ethical conflict that requires a trade-off. But having to choose between her love for her family and her desire to pursue an education is not only emotionally difficult. The trade-off she decides to make will also have important consequences for her success in college and, in turn, for her future. The consequences of either choice are potentially devastating—damage to a meaningful relationship or failing to finish her degree. As we will see in the next chapter, because of the socioeconomic structures into which they are born, strivers are liable to face this kind of tragic conflict more frequently than those who are better off.

A PUZZLE

At this point in the argument you might be wondering: How does a decision in a one-off case like this lead to the sort of ethical costs strivers are liable to pay? Of course, Sandra's choice is difficult, but even if she chooses not to be there for her sister this time, she can make up for it by choosing to help her sick sister on another occasion. When confronted with such conflicts, isn't it possible to balance the competing values by prioritizing one good some of the time and the conflicting good other times? In fact, if we return to Todd's and Henry's stories, we see that they were both trying to pursue something like this strategy. While in college, Todd chose to drive home to visit his family on weekends even though there were many other things he could have been doing on campus instead. And Henry agreed to have his sister stay with him while she was struggling with her addiction even though he was working hard to graduate from college and find a better life for himself. So how is it that Todd and Henry ended up feeling like they had sacrificed those relationships?

There is a genuine puzzle here. As we have seen, one fundamental challenge of the human plight is the struggle to accommodate all of the goods we value within the limitations of a finite life. We all make trade-offs. But a single instance of forgoing a particular good won't make us less engaged with it. It is how we handle these conflicts *over and over again* that determines the people we become. The person who chooses family over competing goods repeatedly is the one who we think of as valuing family. A good friend is not one who only occasionally prioritizes friendship but one who prioritizes it consistently. Cultivating those goods in our life—relationships with family and friends, education, our relationship with our community, our hobbies and interests—requires that we make repeated choices to invest in them. Eventually those small choices add up to genuine engagement.

The puzzle then is that strivers might never feel like they are rejecting or sacrificing family, friends, or community, but they might come to discover after a number of years that they didn't invest enough in those relationships. It is beyond the scope of this book to fully specify what counts as "enough." The answer no doubt varies from individual to individual and is highly context-sensitive. But the point here is that if we really do care about a sibling or a friend, we always feel the pull to prioritize them, even if in some situations we feel that, regrettably, other goods—education, career, or our own wellbeing—must take precedence. And those with whom we have those relationships might, quite understandably, feel rejected or undervalued when we neglect to choose them, especially if we do so over and over again. I will return to this important point later in the book, but it is important to be reminded that the ethical goods we have been discussing—relationships with family and friends and the ties that one feels to one's community—are goods not only for the striver but also for the striver's family, friends, and community. The erosion of these goods is felt by them as well.

The problem is that strivers face ethical conflicts that make it particularly difficult for them to be able to invest enough in all of the areas of their life they value while doing what they need to do to succeed in the path of upward mobility. It is the frequent difficult trade-offs they are forced to make in their circumstances that ultimately weaken their relationships with their families, friends, and communities. This erosion in areas of their life that they find meaningful and valuable can, in turn, affect their sense of who they are.

The High Price Strivers Pay

Let's take stock. I have argued that upward mobility involves ethical costs. These are the sacrifices that strivers make in areas of their lives that are meaningful and valuable—family, connection to community, friendship—which I have called ethical goods. These costs are quite significant because the ethical goods that are at stake are particular and not easily replaced. I have argued that these costs are the result of ethical trade-offs that are made in the face of conflicts between different goods. Sometimes these ethical conflicts are the results of resource limitations that we all face as human beings, but, as we will see, the distinct limitations faced by strivers lead them to confront much more costly and meaningful trade-offs than are faced by more affluent students.

When we tell students to value and prioritize their education, we are in effect telling them to choose education over other competing goods. For those who are fortunate enough to have abundant resources, those competing goods might be time with friends, effort they could expend in pursuing hobbies, or financial resources they might spend on travel. For example, a very well-off student at an extremely selective university is blessed with the option of applying her time and effort toward many potential ethical goods. She still faces many hard choices—choosing between a study abroad program in Italy or a great internship at Google is a hugely consequential choice for this student's future career and her developing identity.[16] But the consequences of her choices are different in two important respects from those strivers face. The first is that the potential negative consequences of her choice

---

16. Thanks to Gina Schouten and to an anonymous referee for pushing me to make this point clearer.

are unlikely to be devastating, as they might be for the striver. A low-income college student who fails out of college is much more likely to stay mired in poverty, saddled with debt. The second key difference is that the costs of the privileged student's choices do not impact her family or community in the same way. A striver who chooses not to play a caretaking role for a sick member of her family in order to attend class has added a significant burden to her already deprived family.

Of course, the majority of students are not either privileged like the student described here or in the dire circumstances many strivers face. Most of them confront situations that are somewhere in between these two extremes. Some middle-class students will incur ethical costs because their families confront a sudden medical or financial emergency. Others might be in better socioeconomic circumstances but still find that their education creates a distance between themselves and those with whom they are close because they are the first in their family to go to college. What the comparison between the privileged student and the striver helps us see is that in order to really understand the ethical costs at stake, we need to look at more than simply the choice being made and take into account the circumstances under which those choices are made. Let's imagine two very different sets of circumstances for Sandra to elucidate this point.

In the circumstances typical of a striver, Sandra faces not only a difficult choice between two aspects of her life that she values, but a situation in which either choice is bad in some important respect for both her and her family—she's either putting her college trajectory at risk or saddling her family with having to find someone to care for her sister. Now imagine Sandra growing up in an upper-middle-class family. Her sister is sick, but she is going to college a few hundred miles from home. If her parents can afford to hire a caretaker to attend to her sister's day-to-day needs, then although Sandra would be just as concerned about her sister, she would experience the conflict between her education and her sister's wellbeing differently.

This comparison illustrates one of the central points of my argument: ethical costs are embedded in larger social, economic, and cultural structures. They do not occur in a vacuum, and they do not affect everyone equally. In the next chapter, with the help of recent work in social science, we will return to this point and situate this phenomenon in concrete social and economic factors—housing segregation, lack of a safety net, and cultural mismatch.

Reconsidering Sandra's Choice

When she came to my office, Sandra was struggling with everything she had to deal with at home and school. She was falling behind in class, but she needed to pass to be on track for graduation. As her professor, I understood my role to be helping her succeed in my class. But, stepping back from that role, I want here to consider the larger ethical question: What should a student like Sandra do? As we have seen, the answer is not as simple as we might have initially thought. Of course, Sandra is in college to get a degree, and doing so, in all likelihood, will make her life substantially better in the long run. With a degree in hand, she might be in a better position to help her family financially after a few years. And if she has taken on debt, it is even more important that she graduate. I strongly believe that this is true for most of my students and other strivers.

But we also need to ask: What is on the other side of that equation? What will she be trading off for the sake of succeeding in college? Those of us who went to college in more fortunate circumstances don't always fully understand what is at stake when students who are otherwise academically capable struggle to graduate. We might interpret such students as irrational or lazy, dismiss their choices as simply the unfortunate product of circumstance, and maybe even conclude that those students do not value education, but rarely do we acknowledge that they might be responding to a genuinely difficult ethical choice. Understanding the broader context in which students are making such decisions should lead us to be wary of drawing such conclusions. If Sandra decides to care for her sick sister, it does not mean that she doesn't care about her education; rather, she has decided that in this instance her family takes priority. Another student in a similar situation might just as reasonably decide to prioritize going to class. These are hard choices.[17] Though these students are making different trade-offs, both are likely to feel guilt and regret once their decision is made because they still value the good they sacrificed.

For strivers, choosing to prioritize their families and communities often means that they risk not finishing their degrees and falling off the trajectory of upward mobility. Students who are fortunate not to face such choices do not value education more; rather, they are lucky to be in circumstances that don't require them to make extremely painful sacrifices in those aspects of their life that matter deeply to them in order to advance their educational goals.

My experience of college was vastly different than that of my students. Yet I relate to some of the challenges strivers face because I was a different kind of striver—an immigrant. When I was growing up, Peru was ravaged by terrorism, poverty, and corruption. My mother and aunt had both emigrated for better opportunities, and my grandmother encouraged me to seek a way out too. I was privileged both in being able to leave and in the manner in which I was able to do it—my aunt and uncle were able to support me financially through college, and I was able to attend a wealthy college that offered me substantial financial aid to cover what my family could not. Despite these advantages, when I immigrated to this country I increased the distance between myself and many aspects of my life that constituted a significant source of meaning and value for me at that time. The sacrifices I made, which pale in comparison to those of students born into disadvantage, paid off

17. For a philosophical discussion of hard choices, see Chang, "Are Hard Choices Cases of Incomparability?" Her TED Talk provides an accessible introduction to her analysis; see "How to Make Hard Choices."

for me in a big way. I can now make a good living and spend most of my hours engaged by work that I find fulfilling and rewarding. But I am ever more distant from my country, my culture, and, crucially, the people I grew up with.

Once we understand the nature of the hard choices faced by strivers, I think we have to resist temptation to judge those who make different choices too harshly. Many Peruvians emigrated for better economic opportunities when I did, but many also decided to stay even when they had the opportunity to leave. They chose to remain close to those whom they loved and to a country and community they cherished. Many of them will readily admit that their economic prospects would have been better if they had gone elsewhere, but they weren't willing to sacrifice much of what they valued for the sake of those opportunities. This was not an unreasonable or irrational choice—there were good reasons on both sides. And it would be preposterous for me to blame my fellow Peruvians who chose to stay, even if as a result their educational or economic achievements were diminished. Yet it is not unusual to hear or read that same sentiment about those who remain in impoverished communities in the United States.

I do not intend to generalize about the motives of those whose lives are marred by lack of economic and educational opportunities. My point is rather that when we seek to understand the ethical conflicts and sacrifices that are so often a part of the story of upward mobility, we should consider the possibility that the choices faced by those born into disadvantage are much more ethically nuanced than we may initially perceive. They are not simply choosing to forsake opportunities for educational and financial advancement; some are choosing to stay engaged with genuinely valuable goods.

As her professor, the best I can do for Sandra is to clearly lay out what is at stake in the options before her. I can advise her about what she can reasonably expect to gain from a college degree. I can tell her how important it is that if she does pursue a degree, she finish it. It would be much worse if she were to drop out with significant amounts of student debt. We can discuss strategies for studying that will help her carve out some time and space to focus on her schoolwork away from home. And I can acknowledge how difficult her choices are. What I should not do is portray a falsely optimistic picture of the path of upward mobility. The narrative we offer strivers should include a true accounting of the ethical costs they might incur to succeed.

2

Situating Ethical Costs in Context

The path of upward mobility is beset with ethical costs—strivers' relationships with family and friends wane, their bonds to their communities weaken, and these changes may even threaten their sense of identity. I've used the term *ethical goods* to refer to those aspects of life that are meaningful and valuable to most of us. I've argued that strivers face ethical conflicts—situations in which one must trade off two or more ethical goods. In the face of such conflicts, strivers incur painful ethical costs. As I argue in the previous chapter, these ethical costs are also borne by those who are left behind—family, friends, and communities.

This experience can be disorienting, and it is all too easy for strivers to see the choices they make and the consequences of those choices as evidence of personal shortcomings. In their book *The Hidden Injuries of Class*, Richard Sennett and Jonathan Cobb describe blue-collar workers who see their achievements and failures through the lens of individual responsibility instead of correctly allocating a significant share of the responsibility to the social and economic structures that undermine their access to the opportunities they seek.[1] Strivers might see themselves as bad siblings, daughters, sons, or friends. They might feel as if their own success has come at the expense of those they love. And, naturally, they might experience surprisingly strong feelings of guilt and regret in light of this perception.[2] The tendency to internalize these ethical costs is understandable, but it ignores the ways in which such costs are closely tied to inequality in the social and economic structures into which strivers are born.

In the previous chapter, I argued that strivers (and their families and communities), because of differences in their background circumstances, face these often-tragic ethical costs differently than do those college students who are better off. These differences are a *contingent* consequence of the particular ways in which unequal access to opportunities and social supports is structured in the United States. That these costs are a consequence of unjust socioeconomic structures means that they can be mitigated by social, economic, and political action. To make this claim persuasive, however, we need to understand how ethical costs depend on the social and economic structures in which we are all embedded. In this chapter, I will draw this crucial connection.

We will look at three factors—socioeconomic and racial segregation, unequal access to social support services and medical care, and cultural mismatch—that play a crucial role in creating and exacerbating the ethical costs that strivers, their families, and their communities face. This is not meant to be an exhaustive list. Rather, I aim to show how we can start drawing critical connections between the difficult experiences of strivers, who are attempting to improve their life prospects through education, and the broader social and economic structures that make those experiences ethically perilous.

The tension between ethical goods and unjust socioeconomic structures is not unique to strivers, though their experience is

---

1. See Sennett and Cobb, *Hidden Injuries of Class.*
2. See Jensen, *Reading Classes.*

distinctive. Women, members of racial minorities, and others who are marginalized by such structures might also experience their own flourishing as being in some ways pitted against the flourishing of the people whom they love. A working mother who feels guilty because she cannot fulfill her commitments at home and at work is in many cases internalizing a conflict that is traceable to social structures that are beyond her control. Increasingly, even those in the American middle class are victims of the same conflict due to the lack of social supports for childcare, medical care, and eldercare.[3] The focus of this book is the distinct experience of strivers, but their predicament reveals a wider phenomenon. The relationships that constitute families, friendships, and communities can be undermined by background conditions of inequality, segregation, discrimination, and lack of social supports. These structures do not neatly divide the population into those who are privileged and those who are disadvantaged, though this is a convenient simplification that allows us to more clearly see the phenomenon. We are all affected to some extent by the factors that we will be discussing.

Jeron's Story: Crabs in a Bucket

Relationships are one of the most important aspects of a meaningful human life. Aristotle argued that human beings are social by nature; we flourish in the company of others.[4] Contemporary philosopher Samuel Scheffler has suggested that our projects and relationships give "purpose and shape to our lives" and thus are a central category of human value.[5] Our development from infancy to adulthood happens primarily through our engagement with the people around us; our friends and family comprise the core of our communities, but even more than that, they are crucial to

---

3. See Collins, "Real Mommy War."
4. Aristotle, "Nichomachean Ethics," 1253a1251–1218.
5. See Scheffler, "Morality and Reasonable Partiality."

our flourishing. Yet for strivers, racial and economic segregation means that those relationships are often in tension with their own flourishing.

We can see this in the story of Jeron*, a young African American man from Texas. When Jeron and I spoke, he was wearing a crisp button-down shirt with a charming bowtie. He looked the part of a college counselor—calm, thoughtful, and affable. Few would guess that Jeron had grown up in extreme poverty. Jeron's mother was a drug addict who had never graduated from high school; in fact, nobody in Jeron's family had. They subsisted off welfare, living in subsidized Section 8 housing in a low-income, predominantly African American and Latino neighborhood in Austin. As Jeron described it to me, their life was "about survival and making sure that you could put food on the table."

When I asked Jeron about the people he grew up with, he said that most of them "are still in the streets selling drugs. Still into the street life." Yet as a child, Jeron was highly dependent on people in his community, particularly because his mother couldn't provide adequate care for him and his older siblings were in and out of jail. When Jeron was in the seventh grade, his chaotic family situation became too much to handle, and he left home. Sometimes he stayed with friends; sometimes he slept on the streets. The family of one of his friends took him in for a bit. During periods when he didn't have a home to stay in, he hid a bucket with all of his possessions behind some bushes each morning on his way to school. In his junior year of high school, his football coach discovered his secret. That moment changed his life. This coach took Jeron in and helped him get into Langston University, a historically black college. After completing a master's degree, he now works for the Department of Residential Living and Learning at a state university in Texas helping other students like himself transition into college.

As a college counselor, Jeron has become even more reflective about what it took for him to succeed. As he described it, one of the more difficult aspects of his path upward had been not allowing himself to be "dragged" back down by those who mattered the most to him—family and friends. He referred to this phenomenon as "crabs in the bucket." Much like a crab trying to claw its way out of a bucket will get dragged back down by other crabs, strivers trying to move upward can be held back and pulled down by those whom they love—even those who have good intentions. Besides one childhood friend who also went to college, most of the people in Jeron's social circle growing up "were going to sell drugs, play ball, join the military, or that was it. Or you die or go to prison." So when Jeron went to college, he disconnected from his community and moved to Oklahoma, because, as he told me, "The only way I felt I could make it through college was if I left completely." Only recently has he started to visit his old neighborhood.

Jeron's story embodies an extreme version of the story of upward mobility. His community was one in which poverty and the challenges that accompany it were severely concentrated and in which avenues for upward mobility were virtually nonexistent. In his situation, those relationships that are meant to be crucial to a person's flourishing became liabilities. Moving up required that he leave them behind.

Finding Opportunities Elsewhere

Jeron's case offers a severe—but all too common—illustration of poverty's consequences. Not all strivers confront situations as extreme as Jeron's. But as we will see in this section, for strivers, opportunities for educational and economic advancement are often found outside of their neighborhoods. Thus, even in cases in which friends and family are supportive and nurturing, moving up the ladder of mobility requires that strivers literally distance themselves from the relationships that would otherwise be central to their flourishing. The distance that they must travel in order to attend college, find a middle-class job, and raise their own kids in a neighborhood with a school that regularly sends graduates to college is literal. But it is also metaphorical—one's own life starts to feel removed from the relationships, concerns, and viewpoints with which one grew up. The amount of distance required can vary a great deal, but negotiating it is often a feature of the experience of upward mobility.

In the United States, a child born into poverty is very likely to live surrounded by others who are in a similar position. Poverty tends to be concentrated in certain neighborhoods—meaning that low-income children will likely live around other families who are poor and go to school with other children who are poor. If those children are Latino or Black, their school is twice as likely to be at least two-thirds low-income than if they are White.[6]

Neighborhoods in which poverty is concentrated tend to have serious problems that make it very difficult for the children who live in them to get a decent K–12 education. For a myriad of reasons—insufficient funding, excessive class sizes, inexperienced teachers, violence, lack of adequate social supports—schools in severely disadvantaged neighborhoods tend to be much worse than those in middle-class neighborhoods. Children who go to these schools are much less likely to graduate (only 68 percent will do so as opposed to 91 percent in low-poverty schools), to attend a four-year college, or to obtain a bachelor's degree.[7] Jeron went to a high school that was typical for someone of his background. It served predominantly low-income students of color. Only about 60 students out of a class of 260 graduated the year that Jeron did. After the Texas Education Agency deemed the school "academically unacceptable" for a number of years, it was shut down.[8] The fact that Jeron graduated from high school is impressive; the fact that he left his neighborhood and went to college is nearly miraculous.

---

6. Orfield et al., "Deepening Segregation"; Orfield, Kucsera, and Siegel-Hawley, "E Pluribus."

7. Bowles, Gintis, and Osborne-Graves, *Unequal Chances*; Aud et al., "Condition of Education."

8. Whittaker, "Johnston High School Is Dead."

The life of a child born into poverty will differ from a middle-class child's life not only in terms of material deprivation, but also in terms of who comprises his or her community and how deeply embedded that child is within the community. Given the reality of socioeconomic segregation, a child born into poverty is going to develop those crucial initial relationships with others who are similarly disadvantaged. In and of itself, there is nothing inherently problematic about this, but, as we will see, concentrated poverty tends to be accompanied by other challenges that threaten the stability of those relationships. Furthermore, children born into poverty aren't only living and going to school with others in a similar position, but are developing deep bonds within their community. Sociologist Annette Lareau, who studies the parenting practices of working-class and middle-class families, finds that working-class parents give their children more freedom and allow them to spend substantial amounts of time playing with other children in the neighborhood and with extended family members.[9] As a consequence, these children tend to be more deeply connected to extended family and other children in their own neighborhoods who are also working class or poor. Middle-class children, in contrast, are more likely to have heavily regulated schedules and to be shuttled between extracurricular activities such as piano class and soccer practice, through which they interact and develop relationships with other middle-class adults and children.

The evidence shows us that children born into poverty tend to live in communities in which poverty is concentrated, attend schools that are plagued by a host of problems, and develop relationships with others who are in a similar position and face similar challenges. But this doesn't establish that there is anything distinctively problematic about the ethical costs that strivers experience in the pursuit of upward mobility. After all, well-educated middle-class kids go away to college and leave their families behind as well. Going thousands of miles away for school is in fact seen as a

9. Lareau, *Unequal Childhoods.*

quintessential part of the American college experience.[10] What is it about economic and racial segregation that makes the distance strivers must travel and the ethical costs they experience distinct?

One crucial difference is that for someone who grows up in a high-poverty neighborhood, leaving one's community is *necessary* to access a good education and, ultimately, a middle-class life in a safe neighborhood with a good school for one's own children. Of course, many middle-class young people leave their communities for a variety of reasons, but most of them do not *have* to do so in order to enjoy a middle-class life; they *choose* to do so. The alternative to leaving—staying near home, maintaining relationships with one's family and friends, remaining a central part of one's community—does not consign them to poverty as it does for strivers like Jeron.

The second key difference between strivers who distance themselves from their families and communities to access opportunities and middle-class children who leave home as part of the college "experience" concerns the consequences of those choices for others. Strivers contribute to their families in a variety of ways— intimacy, mutual care, emotional support, caregiving, and often financial support—and it becomes harder for them to contribute in many of these ways when they leave. In many cases, they also contribute substantially to their communities, whether as a role model for other children, through volunteering, or by simply helping those neighbors who need it. Given that strivers' communities are those in which poverty is concentrated, the people in them depend on each other to provide critical support. Consequently, the ethical costs of a striver's departure fall on communities that are already bearing many other difficult costs. This is not to deny that families and communities may gain from a striver's success, but rather to make the case that there is also a cost of that success to the striver's community, friends, and family, which adds to the challenges they already face. The same is not often true for a child

10. Thanks to Harry Brighouse for raising this point.

from a more privileged community who chooses to go elsewhere for college.

Again, it is important that we remember here that there are a range of ways in which people are affected by socioeconomic segregation. For example, the history of redlining in this country means that racist housing policies might lead to middle-class African American families experiencing challenges similar to those faced by strivers even as their economic position would suggest otherwise.[11]

The discussion thus far suggests that the distance strivers often must travel as they follow the path of upward mobility places a substantial ethical burden on strivers and their communities. But Jeron's story raises a delicate issue that can be turned into an argument against this position. According to him, many of the people he grew up with were involved in crime or with drugs. Isn't the right response to that situation to distance oneself?

We must be careful about generalizing in this context. Jeron's community was—like all communities—composed of people who engaged in criminal behavior and suffered from addiction and mental illness as well as others who were struggling to improve their lives while mired in poverty. We shouldn't paint his community as a hotbed of criminality and drug use. That said, this community was obviously struggling with serious problems.

Let's distinguish two ways in which we might approach the question. In the first, we might argue that given the situation in which he grew up, it was better for Jeron to put distance between himself and his community. Arguably, this was one of the only ways for Jeron to have a better life. But the second perspective on this question, though less immediately practical, is more fundamental, posing an additional question: Should Jeron have to put that distance between himself and those with whom he grew up in order to find a better life for himself? The answer to that question is, I think, clearly no.

11. See Coates, "Case for Reparations."

There is a fundamental problem with a society that pits the individual flourishing of some against their relationships with family, friends, and community. The weakening of these crucial ethical goods isn't a necessary feature of upward mobility. Consider what Jeron's experience would have been had he grown up in a socioeconomically diverse neighborhood. Even if his family was poor, he would not have *had to* distance himself as sharply from his community. His school would have been much better resourced and academically stronger. He would have developed relationships with children and adults from a variety of educational and socioeconomic backgrounds. And if he had had to turn to others for help, he could have found it in those families around him that weren't struggling as much as his family was. It is very unlikely that he would have had to be homeless while in high school. He would have grown up around adults who could have served as professional role models, and his future success wouldn't have been as dependent on a lucky encounter with his football coach.

To be clear, I don't mean to suggest that it would have been better for Jeron to have grown up around different people, but rather that it would have been better if more of the people in his community had been in a better position or if those challenges hadn't been concentrated in his community. Drug abuse, alcoholism, and mental illness affect everyone, wealthy and poor alike, but when a family has the resources to seek the care they need and can rely on other families for support, these crippling problems have a less pernicious effect on the children in that family. Under more favorable socioeconomic circumstances, children who seek to pursue a life away from their communities incur a loss related to that distance, but it is important to recognize that such a choice is fundamentally distinct from that made by a striver. Strivers who choose to sacrifice their ties to their community because it is unlikely that they will escape poverty if they don't are confronted with a tragic choice.

The socioeconomic segregation of neighborhoods has many ill effects on American society.[12] Schools, parks, social services, and other resources in poor communities tend to be worse than those in wealthier communities, and this adds to the deprivation that those who are poor already experience. The lack of access to quality education also means that poor children are much less likely to find opportunities for advancement within their communities. One of the effects of the concentration of disadvantage that is rarely acknowledged is the ethical cost borne by communities when talented members must leave in order to find better lives elsewhere. There are, of course, economic and human capital costs attached to such departures, but there are also other important goods—tight-knit families, friendships, and community bonds—that are potentially weakened or lost.

Carlos's Story: Finding a Way Forward while Living at Home

Jeron had to distance himself from his family and community to succeed. In some ways, he was lucky to be able to do so by going to college at a physical distance from them. Over 60 percent of first-generation college students in the United States live off-campus while they attend college, many with family.[13] Carlos* was a student in one of my political philosophy classes. Dedicated, thoughtful, and eloquent, he was poised to graduate at the end of the semester. He seemed well on his way to a successful career in whatever field he chose. But, as with many of my students, a tumultuous backstory hid not far beneath the surface. When Carlos found out about this book, he got in touch with me, eager to tell me about his experience at CCNY.

12. For a philosophical argument in favor of integration, see Anderson, *Imperative of Integration*.

13. Sallie Mae and Ipsos Public Affairs, *How America Pays for College 2017*.

Carlos had grown up in a heavily Dominican neighborhood. As he described it in an e-mail, the "neighborhood [was] comprised of single mothers, many of whom had little command of English, and many [of] whom held low-wage jobs and relied on government assistance to provide for their children." His mother had raised him and his brother mostly by herself while working as a teller in a Midtown bank. His uncle, who had graduated from college, provided frequent financial and emotional support. With his mother's determination and his uncle's perspective, Carlos was far luckier than many other first-generation Latino students in the United States. But this domestic stability was fragile, and, over a period of years, it fractured. His uncle became addicted to drugs. His mother lost her job and became an alcoholic. And his brother went to prison for rape. Despite this daunting confluence of events, Carlos managed to apply and gain admission to college.

At the City College of New York, Carlos struggled at first. He didn't feel academically well prepared for college. Compounding this difficulty, he lived at home, and the turmoil in his home life only increased while he was in school. During one of his initial semesters at CCNY, Carlos's brother came back from prison. One might think that this would be a positive event in Carlos's life, but it proved far from that. After five years in prison, his brother experienced a drug-induced psychotic break not long after coming home. He was delusional and violent. Carlos felt relieved when his brother was arrested again, but also guilty and ashamed for feeling that way. After this harrowing experience, Carlos became depressed. He also struggled socially at college. He wrote: "I would over-drink at parties because I was awkward. I readily got into arguments and fights, because, after all, I was from the hood and had a gangster for a brother, and so I was not to be out-ranked by condescension." Soon he was in danger of dropping out. Fortunately, he managed to turn things around. He found classes he loved, and a professor arranged an on-campus job that provided stability. He became more engaged with his education. He graduated and found good work as a paralegal. When he contacted me over a year later, he told me that he now had a job of which his mother was proud. He is even able to occasionally help her financially.

Carlos, like the strivers we met in the previous chapter, prevailed over daunting challenges to transform his life. His story is one of odds overcome, a kind of story that we like to hear. We must admire his grit and dedication. That much is clear. Yet it is all too easy to see the obstacles Carlos faced as merely the result of unfortunate circumstances—to think that he persevered against bad luck; that his triumph was to overcome *personal* challenges. In fact, what happened to Carlos was far from a case of bad luck.

Carlos's brother was convicted of a terrible crime, which, if he did commit it, deserved punishment. However, like many other working-class families of color in this country, his experience with the criminal justice system was far from fair. Their family, Carlos noted, "didn't have money to get good or even decent [legal] representation." Carlos's mother used all of their savings to retain a lawyer after his brother's original arrest, but that lawyer, as Carlos described him, was incompetent and ultimately failed to save his brother from prison. More problematically, the prison system did little to help his brother transition into a different life once his sentence was complete. Instead, Carlos's family found themselves dealing with his brother's newly developed mental illness without support. As many families with mentally ill members do, the prison system stepped in to fill the gap left by a lack of mental healthcare, not by getting his brother help so he could rejoin society, but by continuing to imprison him.[14] It is no surprise that Carlos felt like a bad brother for having the complicated set of feelings about his sibling that he did. But we are able to take a step back and see that the responsibility for his brother's situation doesn't lie entirely, or even largely, with Carlos or his family, but with the lack of legal aid and mental healthcare that his family had to reckon with. Reflecting on this would not necessarily have made

14. Torrey, "Jails and Prisons."

Carlos feel less guilty or ashamed, but it might have afforded him a critical distance in a situation in which it was all too tempting to draw a conclusion about himself that gave rise to feelings that threatened to imperil his education.

To see the role that social structures have played in Carlos's story, it is helpful to again imagine him in a situation in which his family enjoyed adequate legal and mental health resources. Even though it would have been stressful for Carlos to know that his brother had committed a heinous crime and that he was suffering from a mental illness, he would have been able to take comfort in knowing that his brother was getting good legal and medical care. Chances are that this would have made Carlos's path through college at least somewhat easier than it was when he had to shoulder a large proportion of the emotional and psychological burden of seeing his mother, uncle, and brother suffer without being able to help them. But it also would have made his mother's, uncle's, and brother's lives better if they had been able to get the help they needed in a timely way. The situation Carlos actually faced was so painful and distressing at least in part because the potential consequences of his choices were so dire. If he distanced himself from his family, he would be taking from them an important source of emotional support. If he failed out of school, his own life prospects would be greatly diminished. Carlos managed to navigate this tricky situation, which is a testament to his perseverance and courage, but the circumstances he faced are not unique.

Caring for Family

For most people, the wellbeing of parents, siblings, children, and spouses plays a significant role in decisions about what to prioritize. Even very young children feel an empathetic impulse to help their caregivers.[15] And as these children mature, those relationships play an ever more important role in supporting their

---

15. Gopnik, Meltzoff, and Kuhl, *Scientist in the Crib*.

transition into adulthood. A strong sense of connection to one's family has been shown to be associated with greater emotional wellbeing and higher educational aspirations.[16] Yet for students from low-income families and from some ethnic groups (e.g., Latinos, Asian Americans), these connections bring with them a particularly strong source of obligation that, when coupled with challenging socioeconomic circumstances, can undermine educational achievement.[17]

In the previous chapter, I argued that part of valuing a relationship is prioritizing the person for whom we care over competing concerns. If a family member is struggling, whether with poor health, unemployment, or a myriad of other needs, a child will feel the pull to do what he or she can to help. Younger children are not in a position to do much in this respect, but when those children approach adolescence, they often become an important source of assistance—helping siblings with homework, caring for elderly relatives, and even contributing financially. And it is precisely when those young adults are poised to enter college that they find themselves faced with navigating both sets of obligations. Focusing on their education often means that they have to abdicate some of the support roles that they play at home. And because of the lack of an adequate social safety net, their families are often in dire need of that support and may be unable to replace it through other means. This leads strivers to face difficult ethical conflicts between their educational ambitions and their desire to support their families.

Susan Sy and Jessica Romero have conducted research among Latina college students from immigrant families that shows the difficulties of maintaining a strong sense of family obligation while pursuing educational achievement.[18] They find that young Latina women are much more likely to understand the goal of

16. Fuligni and Pedersen, "Family Obligation."

17. Sy and Romero, "Family Responsibilities"; Espinoza, "Good Daughter Dilemma."

18. Sy and Romero, "Family Responsibilities."

self-sufficiency through the lens of helping their families financially. Many also see themselves as playing the role of "surrogate"
parent to younger siblings. As they move into college, the nature of
these obligations changes, but, as the authors point out, the attention young Latinas devote to caring for their families can detract
from their focus on their education.

Though the experiences of young Latinas are a particularly
vivid example of the difficulties of feeling torn between caring
for family and doing well in school, the tension is one familiar to
many strivers. Carlos, as we saw, had to reckon with his brother's
imprisonment (and his own sense of relief when his brother was
again removed from his life), as well as his mother's alcoholism and
his uncle's addiction. His family didn't have the resources, legal or
medical, to deal with these challenges. The resulting toll on him
almost led him to drop out of college. In this way, even for those
students who do not play a direct caretaking role, their families'
challenging circumstances are often an important source of tension and worry as they advance through college.

This is not to downplay the importance of gender. Gendered
expectations often burden women with an unequal share of care
work and make it more difficult for them to pursue educational
and career opportunities.[19] The tensions that young female strivers
are likely to feel are further exacerbated by a lack of childcare or
eldercare.[20] Much like social class, patriarchal social and cultural
forces can exact painful ethical costs from women who wish to
transcend the circumstances of their birth. Yet when considering
the role of gender in a young striver's life, we need to tread carefully. The facile recommendation that it would be best for a young
female striver to walk away from her family, reject her culture, or

19. For a controversial but seminal argument about the ways in which multiculturalism and gender equality are in tension, see Okin et al., *Is Multiculturalism Bad
for Women?*

20. Though in some cases, even the availability of such resources is not enough to
get young women "off the hook." Culture does play an important role here. Unfortunately, I cannot fully address it in this book.

resist care expectations should not be made lightly. Carrying out these prescriptions involves a sharp distancing from an important ethical good. The research on Latina college students shows that many of these young women see their obligations not as a demand but as voluntary and a part of their Latina identity.[21] This is not to say that young Latinas and other strivers do not have to negotiate tricky territory, but to characterize the priority they place on family as a hindrance is to fail to appreciate how important familial relationships are to these young people. Unfortunately, this is an issue that deserves much more attention than I am able to offer in this book.

The broader point to bear in mind is that in many cases the reason family becomes a liability in the pursuit of educational opportunities is because there is no safety net for those who need it.[22] Sarah Goldrick-Rab and researchers at the Hope Lab have been studying the hidden costs of college for low-income students.[23] They find that the reported costs of college offer a distorted picture of the actual costs, particularly for low-income families. Financial aid forms, for example, do not consider the contribution that the student could be making to the family's subsistence if he or she wasn't in college. Goldrick-Rab and Kendall write, "Many students from very low-income families make essential financial contributions to their family's wellbeing before going to college. They help pay the rent, transport and care for family members, buy food, and cover medical expenses. Those contributions are reduced when these students reduce their work hours in order to attend college."[24] Though much of Goldrick-Rab and Kendall's

---

21. Sy and Romero, "Family Responsibilities."

22. There are, of course, families that reject a student's educational path on the basis of religious or cultural beliefs. In those cases, the conflicts are coming from a different source than the socioeconomic structures at play, and I don't intend my analysis to apply to them. Most of the stories of strivers discussed in this book are not ones in which this is the case.

23. Goldrick-Rab, *Paying the Price*, is essential reading on this point.

24. Goldrick-Rab and Kendall, "Real Price of College."

work focuses on the financial affordability of college, it also shows us how deeply intertwined familial obligations are with the financial burdens low-income families shoulder in sending a child to college.

It is against the background of a socioeconomic situation in which many families lack adequate social, medical, and financial support that strivers often find themselves called upon to fill in the gaps by providing childcare, eldercare, and even nursing care. Their potential departure is a real cost to a family that might be teetering between staying afloat and sinking into an even more desperate situation. Many families end up relying on their youngest members to contribute because they have few alternatives. The challenge that this poses for the educational achievement of strivers should not be underestimated.

Rhiannon: The Perils of E-mailing the Professor

As we've seen, socioeconomic segregation and the lack of a safety net create situations for strivers that generate painful ethical costs. When I started teaching at City College, I quickly became aware of how these structural factors impacted the lives of my students. I met students who faced housing and food insecurity, who were stressed by medical hardship in their families, and who seemed stretched taut between the obligations of school and those of home. But the other structural factor that I encountered was cultural—students were figuring out how to navigate the norms and expectations of a college campus.

I grant students in my classes three absences throughout the term. I trust them to choose those absences wisely and don't require excuses or doctor's notes. Despite having clearly stated this policy, as class time approaches, my inbox will inevitably fill with excuses—a delayed train, childcare falling through, an unexpected work shift. Many of these e-mails are sent from mobile devices and so are written without the due care that my colleagues and I would expect from a student's e-mail. The informality of these e-mails

rarely surprises me anymore, but when I clicked on Rhiannon's*
e-mail one day, I was in for a shock. In front of me was the image
of a heavily bruised man sitting up in a hospital bed, his head ban-
daged, his expression pained. The hastily written accompanying
e-mail informed me that Rhiannon, who had several absences to
her name already, couldn't make it to class that day because her
sister's boyfriend (pictured) had been in an accident and was in the
hospital. Rhiannon had to be there with him. Questions immediately popped into my head: What happened? Why did Rhiannon
have to be in the hospital instead of her sister? How could she think
it was appropriate to send this gruesome picture to her professor?

Based on the demographics of City College and what we have
discussed here, we can construct a backstory. To be clear, in filling
in the details we are making assumptions that might not be an accu-
rate portrayal of Rhiannon's actual situation—we are constructing
a composite based on what we have learned about strivers so far.
Like many college students from low-income backgrounds, Rhiannon probably lived at home. She clearly felt a strong sense of
family obligation, and it is quite likely that her family struggled in
many of the ways that we have seen strivers' families struggle—
financially, of course, but also with finding adequate healthcare,
caretaking, and social support. And those challenges are ones that
she likely had to contend with on a daily basis in her path through
college. We can already see how they affected her education—she
had already missed more than her allotment of absences and, as is
typical in such situations, was falling behind on her work.

Beyond all of this, the photo and language of her e-mail betrayed
something else—a cultural disconnect between what she thought
was an appropriate way of e-mailing her professor and a widely
held expectation among professors of what an appropriate e-mail
from a student should be. This e-mail didn't make a difference to
her standing in my class; her missing assignments and slipshod
work were the central reasons she was not doing well. But I would
not be surprised if the tone she used in her e-mails affected her
relationships with other professors and administrators. Unlike the

students I taught at Swarthmore before I came to CCNY, many of my current students are often unclear about what constitutes a professional e-mail. Most of the time, I'm grateful for this. I get e-mails that are honest and funny and whimsical. But I do worry that if these students don't learn how to communicate in a way that satisfies the expectations that prevail in professional workplaces, they will be harming their chances at getting into graduate school, securing a good job, or succeeding at an internship. I am now explicit with my students about this. I even have a note on my syllabus about the level of professionalism I expect in their e-mails (e.g., start with "Dear Professor"). E-mail etiquette is only one sign of the cultural mismatch that can exist between some strivers and faculty, administrators, and others in the college community. As we will see in the next section, there is significant evidence that this cultural mismatch is real and can have an effect on a striver's success in college.

Negotiating Cultures

Educational institutions are human institutions with their own set of cultural and social norms. Much of what happens in and out of the classroom is determined by the relationships that teachers, students, counselors, administrators, and staff have with one another. And these relationships are mediated by the social and cultural frameworks of the people involved. In order to succeed in college, strivers have to learn to navigate a whole new social world with a distinct set of norms—ones that many of them haven't been exposed to before they arrive on campus.

When I asked Jeron about the challenges he confronted when he arrived at college, it was clear that he had already given this question a lot of thought: "My social norms, what I thought was standard, isn't standard in the real world," he replied. "You're overly aggressive. You have to defend yourself, because if you don't someone can take from you or you get hurt. So that survival instinct, that defensiveness, I had to learn how to adjust it very quickly in order to excel in a learning environment. I didn't know how to do it." Learning to adapt to college didn't mean just figuring out how to use a bigger library, take notes more effectively, or prioritize paper writing over partying. For Jeron, adaptation required learning how to present himself differently. He had to learn to change his very demeanor, the basic way that he related to other people. He discovered that there was a vast gap between the norms he had grown up with and those he encountered in college. There was, in the words of the social scientists who have studied this phenomenon, a cultural mismatch.

Whenever the word "culture" gets invoked in explanations of poverty, we need to be careful about not feeding into a problematic narrative about poverty that some are all too happy to employ. Some conservative commentators have for decades relished telling young people, often black or brown youths, to hitch up their pants, cut off their dreadlocks, and take responsibility for their future. This narrative about the culture of poverty is sometimes referred to as "respectability politics." Its proponents criticize those from low-income minority communities for holding values and engaging in behavior that they consider counterproductive or self-undermining. The idea, to put none too fine a point on it, is that if only those young people dressed nicely, hit the books, and worked hard, they could lift themselves up into the middle class. Proponents of this kind of critique believe that those who don't make it only have themselves to blame. Such proscriptions are painfully simplistic. As we have already seen, there is plenty of social science evidence indicating that structural factors, such as socioeconomic segregation and lack of social supports, play a much bigger role than individual decisions in entrenching inequality.[25] By invoking culture, I do not intend to endorse the

25. The "culture of poverty" theory can be traced back to the publication in the 1960s of *The Negro Family: The Case for National Action* by social scientist Daniel Patrick Moynihan. In it, Moynihan worries that the breakdown of the traditional family structure was partially to blame for the entrenchment of poverty in Black communities. The report was deployed by many to blame single mothers, "welfare queens," irresponsible

reductive analysis that attributes the entrenchment of inequality to the culture of the poor or to depict that culture as inferior.

But the role of culture must be confronted; ignoring it amounts to neglecting a central challenge for strivers. Part of the problem with the way cultural explanations are often deployed is that they rely on a simplistic idea of what culture is. Culture is portrayed as a monolithic entity—whether of values or norms, of language or style of dress—to which all members of the community, race, ethnicity, or nationality in question subscribe. If we reflect on our own communities, we know that this is absurd.

To start with the obvious, not all Blacks, Latinos, Native Americans, or Whites accept and share the same set of values, norms, linguistic styles, or styles of dress. Nor is it true that culture involves only those factors. Sociologist Ann Swidler, for example, argues for a more expansive understanding of the term, encouraging us to think of culture as a shared framework that we use to understand and approach the world. She suggests that culture encompasses the different habits, repertoires, skills, and styles that people use to interpret and frame their actions.[26] Each of us might employ different cultural frameworks depending on our position in society. For example, a young Latina who is growing up in an inner-city neighborhood is going to share some cultural frameworks with other Latinos, some with other young women, and some with others growing up in neighborhoods like hers. Given the reality that people tend to live in racially and economically segregated neighborhoods, she probably will share many of her frameworks with other young Latinos growing up in the inner city and not as many with upper-middle-class Whites growing up in the suburbs.[27]

---

fathers, and other stereotypical characters who inhabited the "Ghetto" in the public's imagination for various social ills. Poverty, according to this caricature, is the result of "bad" values, laziness, promiscuity, and hedonism.

26. Swidler, "Culture in Action."

27. It is important to note here that frameworks are not values, but rather ways of understanding the world. There might be parts of frameworks that an individual rejects

The cultural mismatch hypothesis argues that there is a difference between the culture that dominates middle-class, often-majority-White, institutions—such as selective universities and corporations—and the cultures prevalent in disadvantaged communities. It doesn't suggest that one is better than the other; rather, it posits that there is a difference between the frameworks that strivers share with others in their communities and the frameworks many in the college community share with each other and with middle-class professionals. So how might this difference be manifested? We've already seen one example in the case of Rhiannon's e-mail. Other examples include ones that Jeron brought up: when and how to make eye contact, how to dress and how to talk, ways of addressing other students or professors, and so on. Sociologists Orlando Patterson and Jacqueline Rivers have studied a program that helps young men from the inner city find jobs. A significant amount of what this program teaches these young men has to do not with job "skills" as we would typically define them, but rather with how to navigate various aspects of self-presentation in a workplace. They have found that those who grow up in the inner city often have an aggressive demeanor that helps them survive in their neighborhoods but hurts their chances of success in a job interview.[28]

But some of the cultural barriers students from disadvantaged backgrounds confront in succeeding in college go much deeper. They concern what to prioritize—family, individual achievement, or financial success—and how to think about the conflicts among these ethical goods. Psychologist Nicole Stephens and her colleagues have conducted a number of studies that support the claim that first-generation college students confront a cultural mismatch when they arrive on a selective college campus.[29] Stephens and her colleagues

---

and others that he or she wholeheartedly identifies with. Cultural frameworks do not determine any one individual's values, preferences, or viewpoint.

28. Patterson and Rivers, "'Try on the Outfit.'"

29. Stephens et al., "Unseen Disadvantage."

argue that first-generation college students often arrive on campus with an interdependent cultural model. According to this model, you understand yourself in relation to the needs and interests of your community. In other words, strivers tend to prioritize precisely those ethical goods that, as we have seen, are likely to come into conflict with educational and career success on the path of upward mobility. In contrast, they suggest, college students whose parents have gone to college and are middle or upper class have an independent cultural model; they understand themselves as independent of others and free to act on their individual preferences and interests. It's not only that such students do not confront the same kind of ethical conflicts as strivers; they are also likely to feel less conflicted because they have grown up with a model in which prioritizing their own individual success over those other ethical goods is encouraged. To add to this, Stephens and her collaborators argue, many selective colleges are organized around the independent model and consequently can be difficult places for students with an interdependent cultural model to navigate. In other words, the culture at college rewards students who are already disposed to prioritize their individual achievement over those other ethical goods.

We should be wary about deploying the cultural model explanation too swiftly without considering the economic background against which these models play out. For example, the cultural model by itself doesn't explain the relative high achievement of Asian American students.[30] It is when an interdependent cultural model, in which family and relationships play a central role, is coupled with difficult financial situations that students are forced to make painful decisions about what to prioritize. What we see then is that socioeconomic challenges, cultural differences, and family obligations collide in a way that makes it difficult for strivers not only to prioritize their education, but also to see college as a place that accommodates and reflects those experiences.

---

30. Stephens suggests that socioeconomic class is more closely related to the difference in cultural models than to ethnic background. For research suggesting that this difference is tied to ethnic background, see Markus and Kitayama, "Culture and the Self."

Of course, the cultural frameworks students use are not static. Students adapt. As they figure out how to succeed in these institutions, students slowly transform to adapt to what is required in that new social context. Sociologist Anthony Jack's work helps us understand how this happens.[31] He has studied two groups of Black students who came from similar low-income backgrounds and were accepted into a selective college but who differed in one crucial respect. One group of students had gone to a private high school through a scholarship program. This group Jack calls the Privileged Poor. The other group had gone to a regular high school. This group he calls the Doubly Disadvantaged. His work offers fascinating insight into the difference that one's social experience before college can make in how one navigates the college experience.

Jack's research suggests that the Privileged Poor students were taught while they attended exclusive private high schools to navigate the culture prevalent at whatever college they ended up attending. They also developed relationships and bonds with students and faculty who were enmeshed in that culture. As a consequence, they ended up finding college much less alienating than disadvantaged students who hadn't had that social educational experience in high school. These Privileged Poor students often remarked on how similar college was to their high school. One of the students explained: "You get in places and you start to feel privileged. Especially with me coming from boarding school. I've already been infected. . . . You get spoiled. You don't even think about it. Sometimes I don't even think of myself as a low-income student."[32]

Such a sentiment was often unimaginable for those strivers who didn't have the advantage of attending private high school. They found college alienating and had trouble forming friendships and relationships with professors. One of them told Jack,

---

31. Jack, "Crisscrossing Boundaries," "Culture Shock Revisited," and "(No) Harm in Asking."

32. Quoted in Jack, "Culture Shock Revisited," 466.

"Freshman year, I didn't say a word. People who I had small classes with, if I see them on the street, I recognize them. They won't recognize me because I didn't speak. My dad would always teach me, 'You don't want to get where you are based on kissing ass, right? You want it based on hard work. It'll take longer, but there's more value to it. You'll feel more proud.' That's bad in *this* context."[33] This difference in how students approach college can have very important consequences for their educational attainment. Going to office hours, developing relationships with other students, and successfully navigating the college culture are important parts of getting a college education. Furthermore, students who are disconnected from campus are more likely to drop out.[34]

Jack argues that the Doubly Disadvantaged experienced a cultural lag until their sophomore or junior year, which had an important effect on their success in college. But what this research also shows us is that students exposed to the culture of middle-class institutions eventually do adapt to the dominant culture.[35] I heard from many of those I interviewed about the "culture shock" of entering college, but also how their eventual transformation affected their friends and family who stayed behind. Jeron told me, "You would think that people would be excited for you, but the truth is that they're not. They're envious in some way because, of course, my body language isn't the same. How I communicate isn't the same. These are my best friends. . . . People that were like my close, close friends have been in and out of the prison system three or four times." Jeron explained that he finds the cool reception he gets at home jarring, but he understands that it is tied to the ways in which he has changed.

The transformation students undergo as they join new communities complicates not only their own sense of where they belong

---

33. Quoted in Jack, "(No) Harm in Asking," 10.

34. Armstrong and Hamilton, *Paying for the Party.*

35. Though some recent work casts doubt on the idea that college students assimilate in this way, it still suggests that those who are closer to the independent cultural model do better academically. See Phillips et al., "Access Is Not Enough."

but also their relationship with those in their communities. In the previous chapter I suggested that ethical goods—relationships we have with family, friends, and our communities—matter to our sense of identity. When those are threatened, so is our sense of ourselves. The cultural element of this transformation further challenges strivers' sense of identity. I do not mean to suggest that there is some norm or presumption that change in this context is "inauthentic," as if there were some static "home" culture from which a striver cannot stray. The point is rather that cultural frameworks mediate our relationships with our families and communities, and, for some strivers, culture is also a valuable part of their identity. When those cultural elements are threatened because a striver's culture is misunderstood or marginalized in college, it can lead to the ethical costs we have been discussing in this book. We will return to this issue in the following chapter.

Who Bears the Ethical Costs of Upward Mobility?

It is important not to lose sight of the fact that there is much that strivers gain from a college education—knowledge and skills, career opportunities, and, if all goes well, a good life filled with ethical goods such as a fulfilling career, friendships, community, and one's own family. In some cases, childhood friends, a striver's community, and his or her family gain as well. A striver who succeeds might be able not only to help those with whom he or she grew up financially, but to provide them mentorship, advice, and help in securing better opportunities. But as we saw in the previous chapter, many strivers are liable to pay a hefty price for their upward mobility. Ethical goods—relationships with family, friendships, bonds with one's community, and one's sense of identity—often come into conflict with what is required to succeed in college and beyond. We all experience conflicts and have to make sometimes painful trade-offs in our lives. But, as I have suggested, the ethical costs that strivers confront are different in two respects. The first is that many strivers *must* bear these ethical costs in aspects of their lives that are profoundly valuable to them in order to be upwardly mobile. The second is that those costs are borne not only by the strivers themselves but also by their families, friends, and communities, who are already disadvantaged in so many other respects.

The evidence presented in this chapter also gives us some indirect sense of how upward mobility affects those who stay behind. If strivers move away to go to college, they are not able to help their families with childcare or eldercare, or to do as much to financially support their families. If strivers live at home while in college, families have to think very carefully about what they can reasonably expect from them or run the risk of undermining their path through college. Friends who rely on each other for advice, support, and inspiration might suffer a loss when a talented friend moves away and that relationship is weakened. And finally, communities lose potentially talented members when the background social structure is such that to pursue a middle-class profession, strivers have to move elsewhere. It is these costs that are often unacknowledged.

When we hear a successful story of upward mobility, we excitedly think about how we can replicate that success with other children. But, as I hope this chapter has made clear, replicating that success does not necessarily help the rest of the community. The success of a handful of students is not a recipe for changing the structural factors that consign those who stay behind to poverty. Upward mobility by itself won't solve issues such as residential segregation, lack of access to social support services and medical care, and cultural mismatch, though in chapter 4 I will argue that strivers are in a unique position to advocate for policy changes that will.

Conservatives are fond of talking about the assault on traditional values by liberal policies. But there is little acknowledgment of the ways in which our most basic values, the ones we all agree on regardless of our political affiliation, are embedded in socioeconomic structures that mean that some people have a much harder time manifesting those values. It is much easier to live up to the values of education, family, and friendship when one grows up in a community with financial and educational resources, in a family that can afford to deal with emergency medical care, or around friends who are not themselves struggling with poverty. We only had to reimagine the lives of any of the strivers we have been discussing under a different set of socioeconomic conditions to see this point. Some might say this is a chicken-or-egg problem: if those people had good values, then they would not be in the socioeconomic situation in which they are. But by focusing on the experiences of strivers, we can see that even for members of disadvantaged communities with the "right" values, there are going to be difficult trade-offs and painful ethical costs. In fact, one might do better in such situations to care less about family, friendship, and community and instead to focus on one's individual gain. When the ways in which we have structured access to opportunities incentivize those unfortunate enough to be born into poverty to disvalue family, friendship, and community, it is time to change those social structures.

3

Navigating an Evolving Identity

When our bonds to family, friends, and community wane and fade, we lose something valuable and meaningful.[1] As we have seen, many strivers must put these important aspects of their lives on the line as they negotiate the path of upward mobility. As significant a risk as this is, it is not the greatest risk that strivers must face. Alongside threats to these important relationships, strivers must confront serious challenges to their own identities.

When I first moved to the United States to attend college, fitting in was a conscious effort. Princeton University in 1998 was a surprisingly diverse place; there were a number of international students, and almost 30 percent of the students identified as minority. But despite this, I wasn't entirely at ease. The stakes for me were high. I was going to one of the best universities in the world, and my family expected me to succeed. I feared being revealed as an

---

1. Many of the central arguments of this chapter are drawn from a previously published paper, "Cultural Code-Switching: Straddling the Achievement Gap," in the *Journal of Political Philosophy*.

outsider, convinced that at any moment I might be exposed as an "admissions mistake." In class, I tried to preempt such an "outing" by declaring my foreignness each time I spoke up, much like some women, worried that they might sound too assertive, preface their own contributions with qualifications and disclaimers. It wasn't easy for me to determine when to try to fit in and when to declare myself an outsider, though I know that my transition was much easier than that of many other international students. In large part this was due to the international American school I attended from the age of five, as well as to a plentiful diet of American sitcoms and movies. Of course, my familiarity with the language was crucial, but knowing all of the characters on *Friends* didn't hurt either.

In most Latin American countries, we use two surnames—the father's followed by the mother's—and I happen to have an Anglo-sounding surname, a vestige from my first stepfather, preceding my mother's Spanish family name. At Princeton, I came to think of them as names for my two selves. Morton became the name of my American self and Galdos the name of my Peruvian self. These two selves were connected but distinct. Once I went to college, Morton became my dominant public self when I lived in the United States, while Galdos sprang to life again on the streets of Lima during those sporadic, and increasingly infrequent, trips home.

As the years passed, I inhabited America more effortlessly. I figured out, without ever realizing it consciously, that assertiveness was rewarded and individuality prized. The longer I lived here, the more those aspects of my personality sharpened into high relief. I learned to negotiate a cramped dorm room with American roommates who didn't seem to think their sheets needed ironing or that perfume was a necessity. I winced when I imagined what my grandmother would think of the piles of unfolded laundry or of our consumption of diet soda by the case. She considered soda a luxury item, only to be consumed when one had guests. But I also became used to the openness and enthusiasm with which virtual strangers would greet me, gradually learning to smile back.

I would return home at least once a year. Once I landed back at Aeropuerto Jorge Chavez, I felt old habits reemerge; the parts of me that remained dormant while I was in America were reawakened. My gender was omnipresent. That category mapped onto different expectations back home. I had to tone down shows of ambition and assertiveness. I had to ignore the near-constant catcalls on the street. When distant cousins came to visit, they all wanted to know what I ate and who I dated, but not what my thesis was about. My grandmother asked me whether I was making Peruvian food for my roommates. She looked disappointed when I admitted I rarely did. People commented on my weight. Living in America, they observed, makes everyone fatter. They didn't think commenting on my weight was out of bounds. Going home wasn't always pleasant, but at the same time I felt an immediate sense of ease in Lima that I only slowly, gradually developed in the United States. Once at home, I knew what the social expectations were, even as I resisted many of them.

I became adept at codeswitching. I came to know what the social norms were in the United States, and as I internalized them, I started to feel less and less foreign. When I went back home, I would slide effortlessly into the social world of Lima's crowded and energetic streets. But as the years passed, I started to feel more at home in the United States and more like a foreigner at home. My sense of identity shifted. Today, I've been living in the United States for 20 years, longer than I lived in Peru. I feel as American as I do Peruvian. Many immigrants will be familiar with the experience of codeswitching as a strategy to succeed in a new country with different social norms while retaining the ability to navigate the social world back home that keeps them connected to their families and countries. Many will also be familiar with the limited extent to which this strategy can be successful in mitigating the changes to one's identity that the experience of immigrating inevitably produces.

In this chapter, we will discuss codeswitching as a strategy for strivers to navigate the ethical conflicts that arise when one is pulled in different directions by conflicting sets of social expectations. Strivers might deploy codeswitching as a way to maintain their ties to their community while adapting to the world in which educational and career opportunities reside. Playing for both sides might be thought of as a strategy to minimize the ethical costs—the weakening of relationships with family, friends, and home communities—that strivers face as they pursue upward mobility. And when one's identity is closely tied to one's family and community, codeswitching may be seen as a way of maintaining that identity as it becomes threatened by the pressure that one might feel to be different at school or at work. But codeswitching can be ethically treacherous. In order to do it with integrity, a codeswitcher must have a clear sense of what he or she values and how much he or she is willing to sacrifice to reach certain goals.

Why Codeswitch?

When President Obama addressed the nation in front of a lectern at the Rose Garden, wearing a crisp white shirt and carefully pressed dark slacks, he sounded like any other Ivy League–educated politician. His race and background seemed incidental to the person standing before the crowd. But when he stood in front of Black audiences, as he did during his 2013 commencement address to the students at Morehouse College, a historically Black university, his presentation and language switched ever so slightly. His race became visible. Obama, as comfortable among White upper-class educated elites as he is in front of a Black congregation, is a master of cultural codeswitching.[2]

The idea of cultural codeswitching is modeled on linguistic codeswitching—which, at its most basic level, is what any multilingual person does when he or she switches from one language to another in response to a change in context. A Latino kid who uses Spanish at home and switches to English at school

2. Beam, "Code Black."

is codeswitching. Cultural codeswitching, by contrast, requires a much more profound shift than toggling between languages or dialects does.[3] It requires that one change how one behaves, talks, and presents oneself as a response to a change in cultural context. Cultural codeswitching cuts closer to the self.

To some extent, we are all codeswitchers. We behave differently at school than we do at work or at a party. Even the Whitest, wealthiest men—those who are most used to the world bending to their whims, rather than the other way around—will likely behave a little differently when they are running a board meeting than they do when they are interacting with their children at home. But for minority students and those from low-income backgrounds, codeswitching involves navigating power dynamics at work or school that put them at a disadvantage.[4] Strivers might feel out of place or even unwelcome if they "reveal" their true selves. The costs of failing to blend in might include losing out on a career or educational opportunity. The pressure on strivers is not merely to switch how they are acting at work or school, but to do so while knowing that the power dynamics are stacked against them.

In chapter 1, we discussed the ethical conflicts faced by strivers. They are often torn between, on the one hand, maintaining deep ties to family, friends, and community and, on the other, pursuing their educational and career goals in the middle-class, largely White institutions where such opportunities are concentrated. This tension gives rise to conflicts that often result in painful ethical costs for such students—losses in those aspects of their lives that are meaningful and valuable to them. As we saw in chapter 2, one of the factors that

3. It is also, of course, employed by children who grow up with two cultures at home. Increasingly, this is true of children from so-called mixed marriages. There is an emerging literature on biculturalism in the psychological and sociological literature. See LaFromboise, Coleman, and Gerton, "Psychological Impact of Biculturalism"; Benet-Martínez et al., "Negotiating Biculturalism Cultural Frame Switching"; Padilla, "Bicultural Social Development"; Nguyen and Benet-Martínez, "Biculturalism Unpacked."

4. Thank you to an anonymous referee for helping me see this point.

contributes to these conflicts is that in many cases there is a cultural mismatch between the world strivers come from and the one that they are trying to enter. Strivers feel pressure to adapt to and internalize the cultural expectations of the White middle class in order to successfully navigate those institutions. Some of these expectations are superficial, but some of them concern ways of acting and cultural frameworks that cut closer to strivers' core commitments and values. Strivers might feel pressure to downplay the importance of family or community or to prioritize their educational trajectory over commitments to friends. In such cases, codeswitching involves aspects of a striver's life that might be extremely valuable to him or her and central to his or her identity.

Sociologists and psychologists have studied the phenomenon of cultural codeswitching—sometimes called "biculturalism"—in a variety of populations. Sociologist Prudence Carter, for example, has studied what she calls cultural straddling in low-income African American and Latino students in Yonkers. Her work provides insight into how students negotiate their school identities in concert with their identities outside of school. One of the young women whom Carter interviewed, Loretta, described the mechanism of codeswitching in this way:

> [If] I'm talking to my friend or father, [I say], like, "Yo, whassup, whatever." When I call my job, I have a different attitude toward the whole situation, you know. I don't talk with slang. I make sure everything is correct. But I don't know. Me personally, I think . . . [f]or a Black person to "act white," like when he arrives [at home] I think he don't have to do that. But, like, even if he's in school, he can like that in a school. Maybe it'll get him somewhere. You know? And when he go out or whatever he don't have . . . I don't know . . . they don't have to act like that. You can just be yourself. But there it is, it is going to be times in your life when [you] are going to have to put on a little act, or a little show to get the extra budge or whatever, you know.[5]

5. Quoted in Carter, *Keepin' It Real*, 60.

Loretta here offers a knowing analysis of the complex work she is doing. Codeswitching involves "putting on an act" in order to make it more likely that one will succeed at work or school. But it is also clear from the way she talks that codeswitching always comes with the risk of inauthenticity, particularly for someone who is Black. She can't understand why someone would, in her words, "act White" at home. That "act" should be reserved for contexts in which it is required for success. Her implicit rejection of "acting White" suggests that Loretta believes that for someone who is Black, acting in such a way is, by definition, not authentic. Codeswitching is a strategy for succeeding at work or school, but also one that Loretta deploys to preserve a sense of identity that is set apart from those spaces. It is both a way of fitting in with a community in which one sees oneself as an outsider and a way of pushing back on the pressure to change one's identity to become more like those who reside in that community.

Cultural codeswitching seems to offer a neat solution to the conflicting demands that strivers confront. Failing to adopt this strategy can result in fraught social interactions or even harm one's educational or economic outcomes. The ability to switch how one acts and present oneself in two different contexts—one's home community and those places in which opportunities for educational and career advancement are found—appears to offer the best of both worlds. And for those students who value aspects of their identity that are closely tied to their home community, codeswitching can be a strategy to push back against pressures that might otherwise compel them to sacrifice those aspects of their identity.

Gabriela's Story: Learning to Fit In

Gabriela* grew up in Newark, New Jersey, and graduated from Princeton a little over a year before our interview took place. She is half-Brazilian—her mom was an immigrant—but grew up with her White father after her parents' divorce. They struggled financially.

Her father was unemployed for long stretches of time. Sometimes they had no heat in the winter. Gabriela attended a Catholic school in Elizabeth, New Jersey, on a full scholarship. The school was safe, but it wasn't like the kind of private schools that many of her classmates at Princeton had attended. It was majority non-White, and it didn't regularly send students to highly selective colleges.

Gabriela had a rough first semester. She didn't get adequate advising, took too many courses, and struggled academically. She told me that she internalized the "idea that [she] wasn't good enough . . . that [she] was an affirmative action admit or that [she] wasn't smart enough to be there . . . an admissions mistake." She felt that others saw her as a token—that she was there to "represent minorities" and so she had to work extra hard to prove that she was as good as everyone else. Despite these initial challenges, Gabriela flourished. She joined two very different groups—the women's rugby team, which she described as more diverse in a variety of ways than the general population at Princeton, and a sorority, which provided a different kind of female bonding experience. These groups and a professor who "went out of his way to remind [her] that she deserved to be at Princeton" provided crucial support and guidance.

Even as she became more and more integrated into a diverse set of new social networks, Gabriela still went back home often, especially when her grandmother fell ill. In her senior year, when her grandmother's health deteriorated further, Gabriela lived at home at the beginning of the semester. She drove to school early in the morning to take classes and back home in the evening—an experience that probably very few of her classmates were having in their last year of college. Her relationship with her home community was complicated. She told me: "I get a lot of judgment from the community . . . just because they couldn't understand my ambitions, people who didn't understand why I didn't come home from college every weekend, didn't understand why I wanted to study, didn't understand why I would study something stupid like politics."

Yet Gabriela wasn't entirely comfortable with the social life at Princeton either. The undergraduate experience at Princeton has long been dominated by eating clubs, controversial co-ed social and dining clubs that have been part of the university's history since the nineteenth century. Gabriela hated the eating club system. And the university itself has viewed the clubs critically, suggesting in a 2010 report that "the clubs . . . continue to be a polarizing force, for reasons that seem to derive in part from a social stratification that persists despite a number of efforts to ameliorate it, with students from lower-income families and minority groups participating less fully in the clubs than other students."[6] But despite Gabriela's well-founded dislike of the eating clubs, she still joined one, feeling that it was important to have a club on her résumé when she went out on the job market. The alternative, being an "independent" (the name given to those who are not members of eating clubs at Princeton), meant in her view: "You're poor. Everyone knows it. Nobody wants to talk about it . . . but having that club on my résumé is going to have political payoffs later on."

Gabriela became adept at navigating both worlds during college. But when I asked her about her community now, she found it hard to identify one. She no longer went back home; her grandmother had passed away, and her father had moved abroad. She told me she was comfortable among the other college graduates in her internship program but felt particularly close to her roommate, the only other minority. They were able to talk about their experiences in a way that she could not with some of the other people in the program. But she wasn't entirely sure how she felt about the ease with which she now fit in with her group of college-educated coworkers. She often discussed this with her roommate, wondering whether they were more at ease because of "assimilation and becoming comfortable with being a minority or getting tired of pushing back and demanding to be treated

---

6. Trustees of Princeton University, *Report of the Task Force*.

better . . . [or] how much of it is actual improvements." As we will see, the questions that Gabriela and her roommate are contending with here—How am I changing? And, crucially, why?—are at the heart of the codeswitching experience for strivers.

A Divided Self

Not all of the changes a striver experiences are the product of trying to fit in or adapt to one's new social world. Education is supposed to transform us. Reading Plato and Gabriel García Márquez, spending weeks mating fruit flies to watch selection at work, making new friends, gaining expertise and the confidence that comes from it—all of these experiences have the potential to change us in deep and profound ways. It should come as no surprise that we emerge from college different people. Yet other changes can seem disingenuous or inauthentic. Strivers might feel like they are capitulating to the social norms and expectations of a new context simply because it is easier to accede to those in power, not because they really come to see the value of a new way of being or acting. For some, joining an eating club or fraternity might feel like this kind of capitulation. The experience of upward mobility is complicated in part because it is sometimes difficult to tell why or how one is changing.

Yet we should be wary of thinking of this issue as one concerning authenticity. If authenticity is thought of as staying true to one's childhood self or to a particular culture, then most education will be inauthentic. Education, ideally, should lead us to reflect on and be critical of our beliefs. In light of this reflection, we might reject some of our beliefs for good reason. Furthermore, many strivers welcome the changes that upward mobility brings. The question is not whether a striver is changing, but whether those changes are in harmony or tension with a striver's relationships, values, and other central aspects of life that matter to him or her. As we will see, codeswitching doesn't offer a straightforward way out of this bind.

It might be tempting to think of codeswitching as a divide-and-conquer strategy—a dividing of the self into two, in which one self adapts and succeeds in the world of middle-class institutions and another remains rooted in family and community. But are there not consequences that stem from dividing oneself in this way? Is it a good way of mitigating some of the ethical costs often required by upward mobility? What effect might codeswitching in this way have on one's identity? To explore these questions, let's consider a hypothetical case.

Imagine that you grew up in a loving Latino family that was deeply Catholic and hovering near the poverty line. Your neighborhood was composed of other, mostly poor Black and Latino families; you all shared a lack of access to good schools, public transportation, and other basic community resources. Somehow, you managed to succeed at your dismal school, win a scholarship to the local state university, attend law school, and become a successful lawyer at a prestigious law firm. You moved to an upscale neighborhood closer to your office and developed friendships with other middle-class professionals and college graduates.

Yet you still seek to maintain your connection with your family and the community in which you grew up. You try hard to go back home every Sunday for church and dinner with your parents. You dutifully attend the *quinceañera* celebrations of your many cousins as they each turn 15. You go to the old cafe to chat with your neighbors. Each time you go back home, your demeanor, clothing, language, and interests shift to fit in with those of the people with whom you grew up. You talk with the neighbors about the latest *telenovela* on Univision, speak Spanglish, complain about how expensive everything is these days, and devour the deliciously spicy food your *abuela* makes. When you're back at work, you switch back to your professional role. You fit in with the norms of a corporate workplace: you talk about the articles you read in the *Wall Street Journal* on your way to the office, you speak Standard English, you discuss your retirement investments, and at lunch you choose the kale salad over the Cuban sandwich. In other words, you codeswitch.

One way of conceiving what you are up to here is that you have divided yourself into distinct, compartmentalized selves. You have a Latino, or family, or neighborhood self. And you have a work, or professional, or "bougie" self. In this way, you can have it all: a relationship with family and community, a successful career, a nice middle-class life. You have divided, but have you succeeded?

There are two problems with this strategy. The first is that it is unstable. Challenges, both expected and unexpected, will inevitably bubble up. Conflicts are unavoidable. A grandparent gets sick; your sister loses her job; your firm requires that you travel most weekends; the partners at your firm eye you with suspicion. You ultimately cannot avoid conflicts by dividing yourself up—or at least you cannot avoid conflicts forever. When your sister calls you at work to tell you that she needs help because she lost her job or because your grandmother is sick, you can't just say: "I'm sorry, right now I'm in professional mode. I'll deal with it whenever I make it home." This is because, as we discussed in chapter 1, part of what it means to value family and relationships is to give them priority when that is what is called for. Your sister might try to be understanding, but she will still be upset if you prioritize your work over your grandmother. On the other hand, your performance at your job, along with your chances of being promoted, might suffer if you simply leave work in the middle of the day or refuse to travel on weekends. Your employer's demands can, and for many do, conflict with those other parts of your life. And you might feel quite powerless to refuse your employer's demands or nervous about sharing the real reasons why you can't meet them.

In her book *Reading Classes* psychologist Barbara Jensen offers a devastating portrait of the psychological anguish and stress that working-class people who have succeeded in the path of upward mobility experience as they straddle both worlds.[7] Jensen tells the stories, including her own, of those who, having grown up working class, end up feeling not simply that they are divided between

7. Jensen, *Reading Classes*.

cultures, but that their home culture is disrespected and devalued by those in the middle-class worlds they now inhabit. And here we encounter a second, related problem. The dilemma confronting strivers is not only psychological, but ethical. Even though you might feel as if you are two different people, you are one person on whom both family and work are making demands. Your family has a relationship with *you*, not with your "family self." Your boss wants *you*, and not just your "work self," to prioritize work. Both your professional commitments and your personal relationships make their demands not on just one of your selves, but on you as a unified person. These competing demands threaten to split you into two, but this threat to your identity cannot be mitigated by simply accepting this division as who you are.

Compartmentalizing in this way is a precarious and unstable way to codeswitch. It seeks to avoid genuine ethical conflicts that are often unavoidable. Furthermore, it doesn't give us a useful vantage point from which to decide what to do in cases of conflict. Your "family self" may think you should go visit your grandmother, while your "work self" may think you should stay at work, but which self is the one who is going to decide? In trying to divide oneself in this way to avoid ethical costs, one does lose something—the unified vantage point that is so central to how most of us see ourselves. Depending on codeswitching to avoid deciding between competing values, relationships, and commitments only delays and postpones the difficult but necessary work of choosing for oneself which of these goods are most meaningful.

Faking It without Becoming It

Instead of thinking of codeswitching as dividing the self, strivers might decide to shield a part of themselves by putting on an act in those situations in which acting as they would normally might come with a cost—a job interview, a graduate seminar, a networking dinner. Loretta's explanation of the ways in which she negotiates this type of situation seems to follow this model.

In this way of understanding codeswitching, your "real" self, the one that manifests itself at home, is masked at work or at school by a "pretend" self. One of these selves is your authentic, unified self, and the other is a performance put on for pragmatic reasons.[8] In this way of thinking about codeswitching, you are protecting your identity from the pressure to conform to a community by pretending instead of really changing.

So let's amend our imagined story in light of this approach. Here, when you go to work you are putting on your professional face to fit in and to successfully navigate your corporate law firm. You act as if you love kale salad and the *Wall Street Journal*, and that the thing you care the most about is making partner. Yet the real you is the one at home, the one who emerges when you take off your business suit at the end of the day, the one who watches *telenovelas* and loves *chicharron*. Instead of moving to the upper-middle-class neighborhood near your office, you move closer to where you grew up. You see the self who goes to work as a performance and your real self as the one who comes home to *El Barrio*.

But this approach doesn't get it quite right either. Seeing your work or school self as a pretense doesn't shield you from the ethical conflicts we've discussed. When your sister calls you at work or while you're at school, telling her that you are in *pretend* work mode is not going to appease her any more than telling her that you are being your "professional self" will. We don't get around those conflicts by pretending.

More problematically, this strategy seems to threaten your ethical integrity, not because you are acting inauthentically, but because you are not taking responsibility for your behavior. If you are putting on an act in which you portray yourself as career driven, competitive, or cutthroat for many hours a day, at some

---

8. Some sociologists, psychologists, and philosophers have thought that, in fact, all of us are always performing. According to this view, there is no real self that is authentic. Though interesting, this view has problems accounting for the phenomenological distinction between the "real" self and the "fake" self that many do feel. See Goffman, *Presentation of Self*; Velleman, *How We Get Along*.

point you have to ask yourself: Isn't that at least part of who you are? Putting on an act might be a way of dealing with an uncomfortable situation every so often, but seeing hours of your day as an act involves not taking responsibility for your actions. After all, the person who is doing all of these things is you. You are not an actor in a theater. To resist the threat to one's identity by assuming this posture is to capitulate while pretending that one hasn't.

In her brilliant book *The Managed Heart*, sociologist Arlie Hochschild studied Delta flight attendants in the early 1980s. These flight attendants were taught to manage and withhold their normal human emotional reactions to someone being rude and nasty. Instead, they were supposed to remain calm, to act nice, and to greet everyone with a smile—in other words, to put on a performance. What Hochschild found is that after hours of doing this kind of emotional work, the flight attendants had difficulty switching back to "normal" at home. This insight illustrates the central problem with seeing the self who goes to work or school as merely a performance and not truly a part of who we are. The performance can be hard to shake. It might be psychologically necessary to see our other self as not the "real" us in order to contend with the demands of work or school, but we cannot entirely prevent that performance from affecting who we are and how others see us over time.

But the problem is not merely psychological; it is also ethical. Let me offer an example from my own experience to illustrate this point. Academic philosophy, my field, is disproportionately White and male, more so than other humanities departments and even more so than some hard sciences like chemistry. The culture of philosophy is also very sharp and argumentative. The goal, as some see it, is to tear another person's argument down by punching as many holes through it as one can. As an undergraduate, I quickly picked up that this was what I was supposed to do. At first, I saw this as a kind of performance—a "philosophy mode"—that was expected in the seminar room. It was not until years later, after a friend called me out for asking questions too aggressively during a seminar, that I realized that this act had become who I was even though it was not who I wanted to be. I'm grateful to my friend for criticizing my behavior, because I was contributing to an academic culture I despise. To hold up my hands and feign innocence and say, "I was just pretending" would have been a cop out. I had become part of a problem by shielding a part of myself from self-criticism. I've struggled to unlearn this behavior, though in many philosophy contexts such aggression is still rewarded, making it all the more difficult to change.

Most of us have heard the phrase "fake it 'til you make it," meaning that by forcing yourself to behave in a certain way enough of the time, eventually you will change such that the behavior that felt fake at first will come to feel natural. Suppress your self-doubt, act confidently, and eventually you will feel confident. The idea of codeswitching as pretense suggests that one can pretend in order to shield oneself from changing. The thought is that you can "fake it" as a corporate lawyer without ever really "selling out," even though you are spending most of your day working toward the driven, career-obsessed ideal that your colleagues uphold. And, most importantly for our purposes, this position assumes that the real you can remain connected to your community even while the "pretend" self who is going to college or working prioritizes that community less and less.

Yet what we do day after day ultimately reflects what we value. As I argued in chapter 1, it is the choices that we make over and over again that add up to genuine engagement with the people, communities, and projects that matter to us. Of course, many of us are forced, while at work or school, to act in ways that we wish we didn't have to. And strivers are often justified in doing so, especially when they are trying to make it in spaces that are inhospitable to those without privilege. Research by sociologist Lauren Rivera substantiates Gabriela's perception that her participation in an eating club would benefit her in job interviews. Employers in corporate law, finance, and consulting often do look for those "signifiers" that are closely tied to class in deciding who to hire.[9]

9. Rivera, *Pedigree.*

Consequently, her decision to join an eating club, despite rejecting what they signified, was a good strategy to improve her chances of getting hired in one of those industries.

While there is something appealing about the pretense model of codeswitching in circumstances in which being genuine will put one at a disadvantage, there is also something deeply problematic about it. To see how one acts during many hours a day as merely a performance fails to contend head-on with the ethical challenges that codeswitching poses. Strivers need to engage in honest reflection when confronting the pressure to change in ways that potentially harm their ability to stay connected to their family, friends, and community.

The Perils of Codeswitching

As we have seen, codeswitching through division or pretense is ethically problematic. Both of these strategies allow strivers to avoid figuring out where they stand when faced with a clash between the two worlds they are inhabiting. And, as I have suggested, these conflicts can also threaten fundamental aspects of our identity. If we are not reflective about how we respond to them, we risk changing in ways that we don't endorse. Politics provides us with an apt comparison. Politicians like President Obama are often master codeswitchers. They know how to read an audience and adapt their behavior to suit it. This chameleon-like ability to adjust to an audience is a skill that makes a politician more likely to succeed. But a politician who too easily caters to the audience, saying one thing one day and the opposite the next, inspires distrust because we don't know where he or she stands. We're not entirely sure of who he or she really is.

Consider how difficult it was for Hillary Clinton to gain voter trust during the 2016 presidential campaign. Clinton can appear overly rehearsed—ready to say whatever will suit the political context. Yet, according to reporting by Ezra Klein for *Vox*, people close to her say they trust her and that she is not as she appears in the public eye. Klein suggests that this is because Clinton "is a master compartmentalizer, and she believes she can cleave who she is on the campaign trail, and who she is in the minds of Republican voters and even some Republican politicians, from who she'll be as president."[10] An unfortunate side effect of masterfully compartmentalizing in this way is that people end up being unsure of what your perspective really is.

When politicians are too smooth, too willing to change how they act and what they say to suit the political context, we worry that they lack an ethical backbone. We fear that we don't know what they truly stand for. Yet refusing to engage in any political codeswitching makes the path to victory that much harder. To successfully win an election or pass a law that a politician really believes in, he or she has to be flexible enough to understand what the political context requires and make some compromises. Politicians have to tread this difficult boundary—successfully adapting to a given political context without sacrificing their principles or values—in order to pursue the goals that really matter to them.

The same is true, I suggest, of strivers who have to navigate the middle-class spaces where opportunities reside. Blindly changing to suit the context might make one more successful in achieving certain educational or career opportunities, but in doing so one risks losing one's ethical backbone. There are certain values that matter to each of us and are important aspects of our identity, whether these are particular friendships, relationships to some members of our family, or ties to a particular community and the culture that is a part of it. In changing or concealing those aspects of ourselves unreflectively, we risk incurring ethical costs we may later regret and becoming people we don't want to be. On the other hand, refusing to change at all to suit one's context can make the path toward success incredibly difficult. For strivers, who are already in a vulnerable position socioeconomically, this is a very risky option.

10. Klein, "Understanding Hillary."

The ethical challenge lies in striking a balance between resisting the pressure to adopt the dominant cultural norms when those conflict with our values and being flexible enough to adapt and thrive in that culture. As we have seen, neither dividing the self nor pretending is a viable strategy. What we need is a way to codeswitch that allows us to be clear about what matters to us—that allows us to define and articulate our values—and that thus helps us thread the needle between blind assimilation and equally blind resistance. When there is so much pressure to fit in in order to succeed, taking control of those aspects of our identity that matter to us requires reflection.

Race and Gender

Before we turn to what I will argue is the most fruitful model for dealing with the ethical conflicts faced by strivers, we must briefly discuss the ways in which race and gender impact codeswitching.[11] Unfortunately, I cannot give this topic the attention it is due in this book, but it is an important one to keep in mind. Given the links between education, class, and race in the United States, many strivers are racial minorities, particularly Blacks and Latinos. And given the caretaking expectations that our culture has of women and hostility to those who don't fit into gender categories, many female and nonbinary strivers have different expectations foisted on them than their male counterparts encounter.[12]

An idea very similar to codeswitching has been a part of racial analysis ever since the late nineteenth century, when W.E.B. Du

11. There are many other categories of oppression that could be discussed in this context, including sexual orientation and ability status, to name but a few examples. Unfortunately, there is not enough space in this book to consider those categories with the due care they deserve.

12. In what follows I discuss women as a central example of an oppressed gender category. In doing so, I do not mean to exclude trans or nonbinary people. To do justice to this issue, more would need to be said about the impact of these various identities on strivers.

Bois, the African American writer (and sociologist), coined the notion of "double-consciousness" to describe the African American experience:

> It is a peculiar sensation, this double-consciousness . . . two souls, two thoughts, two unreconciled strivings; two warring ideals in one dark body, whose dogged strength alone keeps it from being torn asunder. The history of the American Negro is the history of this strife—this longing to attain a self-conscious manhood, to merge his double self into a better and truer self. In this merging he wishes neither of the older selves to be lost. . . . He simply wishes to make it possible for a man to be both a Negro and an American, without being cursed and spit upon by his fellows, without having the doors of Opportunity closed roughly in his face.[13]

This sounds very much like the notion of cultural codeswitching we have been investigating—the idea of having two selves with two distinct souls, thoughts, and ideals. I do not intend to offer an analysis of double-consciousness here, but Du Bois's perceptive passage points us to some of the key ways in which codeswitching is different when one is a member of a racial minority or of an oppressed gender category.

The first key difference is that both gender and race are social categories that carry with them the stain of prejudice and discrimination.[14] A person who is racialized—someone whose behavior, capacities, and intelligence are thought to be tied to his or her racial status—has to not only adapt to the expectations of the cultural context he or she is in, but also take into account what stereotypes are influencing how he or she is being perceived by virtue of his or her skin color. The same is true of gender. Someone who is perceived as a woman has to consider, in addition to any

13. Du Bois, "Strivings of the Negro People."
14. For more on this issue, see Appiah, "Race, Culture, Identity"; Haslanger, "Gender and Race."

challenges she confronts on the basis of her family background or class, how her perceived gender is influencing the expectations that others have of her skills, social role, or worth. Consequently, the power dynamics at play for a striver engaged in the path of upward mobility are further compounded by racial and gender oppression.

This leads to a second key difference. The limits of how successfully one can codeswitch depend on the attitudes toward race and gender that are dominant in a particular social context. Someone who is Black in a context in which people have very strong racist attitudes—for example, the Jim Crow South—would not be able to act as a member of the dominant class. His race would be omnipresent no matter how much his language, dress, and cultural attitudes were aligned with those of the dominant class. The situation would be different if he was in Brazil, where he would still be racialized, but using different categories. And it would be different still in contemporary America. The case is not dissimilar for a woman, who also has to think about how perceptions of gender will delimit how successfully she can codeswitch. In some contexts, for example, acting as confident as one of her male colleagues might backfire because she is likely to be perceived as too aggressive. In other contexts, showing that she cares for her family might lead to others perceiving her as less serious about work. In both the case of race and that of gender, codeswitchers have to not only master the norms that structure the new social world they are trying to enter but also become intimately familiar with the predominant stereotypes that will determine how they are seen in this world, knowing full well that their race or gender (and, in some cases, both, of course) might limit how far they can successfully codeswitch.

A final key difference is that for members of oppressed groups, codeswitching can be seen as a betrayal of one's community. Loretta hinted at this when she criticized someone who acted "White" at home. Codeswitching can be seen as a way of capitulating to stereotypes and expectations that are unjust and racist.

I am not suggesting by any means that thinking of codeswitching as a betrayal is right; rather, I am observing that there is a risk that one's community might see it as such. Thus, the likelihood of such a reaction from a codeswitcher's home community means that he or she has to bear this potential cost in mind. The case of gender is much more complicated on this score, since gender cuts across communities in different ways than race does. However, a woman might worry about how she is being perceived not only by the community at large, but in particular by other women who are navigating a similar set of challenges. Unfortunately, there is so much more to be said about the relationship between race, gender, and codeswitching than we have space for here, but it is important to be reminded of the additional layers that codeswitching requires for strivers whose other identities are sources of further prejudice and marginalization.

Lucy's Story: Race in Rural America

The complexities of race were omnipresent for Lucy*, who grew up in a rural town in the South being perceived as White. She came from a family of farmers and learned to farm very early on. Her mother was half Cherokee, but this was hardly discussed or mentioned. Her mother chose to pass as White, and Lucy's community was composed mainly of low-income White rural farmers. Lucy recalls that "to survive in the South, to survive in a rural place, wherever, whenever a racist joke is told, the best you can do is just not say anything or just smile, but not say anything. I always had this thing of like, 'If you're saying all these jokes about why it's funny to kill Black people and to kill Natives, what would you really think if you knew who I really was?'" Through an agriculture-related extracurricular group at her school, Lucy met a professor who convinced her to apply to college. She went off to Murray State University, where she encountered students from more privileged backgrounds. Her relative lack of privilege left her feeling lonely and unable "to say who I was or why I don't spend money on things." Graduate school in the Northwest was even more alienating. She felt that the professors didn't know how to interact with students from her background. What made her most upset was that she was in an environmental studies program in which the other students and professors romanticized signifiers of the kind of farming life that she had actually grown up having, yet they were dismissive of her perspective.

Despite these challenges, Lucy finished her master's degree and had, when I interviewed her, recently returned home to work with an organization that encourages environmentally sustainable community-based farming. She saw herself as a mediator: "That was a role I took on myself that I knew would alienate both worlds if I didn't have a foot in both worlds." Even though her family supports her work and the goals of her organization, her unwillingness to tolerate racism has been a source of strain. "Whenever I say, 'Halloween makes me really mad because everyone's walking around in blackface and headdresses,' she [Lucy's mother] is just like, 'You are part of the problem. You're the PC police,'" she recounted. As Lucy told me about these interactions, she was on the verge of tears. The gulf separating her from her mother was painful, but she also rejected the idea that she should simply go along with racist comments just to get along.

Lucy's attitudes toward race had changed gradually as she was exposed to a diversity of people and perspectives in college and graduate school. She was glad that she no longer held racist views. But after coming back home, she was confronted with the pressure to pretend that she hadn't changed in this way, though many respected the expertise she brought to their community. Lucy had to codeswitch to convince the farmers in her community to take her seriously. Her work depended on the strength of those relationships. And she was able to successfully act as a bridge between her organization and those farmers, but going along with racist attitudes was a step too far. It would involve sacrificing a part of her new identity that she valued. Lucy was engaging in what I will call clear-eyed codeswitching.

Clear-Eyed Codeswitching

The divide-and-conquer and pretense strategies are ways of trying to keep different worlds from colliding. The motivation for these two models is clear. One wants to be able to succeed at work or at school even when what is demanded from us feels at odds with who we see ourselves as being. I want to be a successful philosopher even though often I feel uncomfortable and out of place in this largely White, male field. Seeing that self—the one who does philosophy—as a different, other self or as an act is, as I have suggested, an unstable and ethically problematic way to contend with that challenge.

What we need is a way to deal with the threats to what we value and our identities in an honest and reflective way. We need to take responsibility for the self who inhabits the various spaces in which we live by being clear about what we're up to when we are codeswitching. This doesn't mean that we can't sometimes compromise or end up acting in ways that feel at odds with who we are. But we need to be reflective about what we are sacrificing and why. Is it worth staying silent when one hears racial slurs for the sake of getting along? For Lucy, it is not. Staying silent requires that she go against a deeply held belief. It threatens her ethical integrity. But perhaps joking about hipsters, who love food in Mason jars but have never set foot on a farm, is something she can do even if it doesn't feel completely aligned with her new view of the world. Like many strivers, Lucy has to chart a difficult course in order to do her job well, maintain her relationship with her community, and be true to what she believes.

To codeswitch in a way that is honest, strivers have to figure out where to draw the boundaries. But to do that strivers need to be reflective, which is neither easy nor automatic. Few of us want to have an argument with our family about race or feel obligated to push back when our boss asks us to work overtime, even if it conflicts with our family obligations. And it is in those moments that we often end up compromising on something that matters to us—maybe we end up forgetting to check in with our sick cousin, or we agree to go on a work trip when we're supposed to be home celebrating our *abuela*'s birthday, or we let a racist comment at work slide because it's too hard to stand up to it. This is why finding the time to engage in this kind of ethical reflection is important. It is through reflection that we can become clear on what matters to us and why.

As we will discuss in chapter 5, studies show that values affirmation—in which students are asked to reflect on what they value before taking a test—reduces some dimensions of the educational achievement gap between minority and White students.[15] But reflecting on what we value is not only important because it might help us achieve better scores on a test. Reflecting on what matters to us—family, friendships, communities—gives us a tool to push back against social structures that, as we saw in the previous chapter, constantly threaten to undermine those ethical goods. Unreflective codeswitching, as I have suggested, can leave us unmoored—pushed this way and that by circumstance. We take the easiest route and end up feeling that we gave something up without meaning to. We don't recognize the selves who emerge as the people we want to be.

If codeswitching is to be valuable, it should enable us to lead lives that are full of those ethical goods we have talked about—family, friendship, and community. Sometimes, it is worth it to adapt to the context for the sake of goals we care about. But other times, adapting can lead us to lose a sense of who we are and what we care about. When a friend chides us for being too aggressive, when a family member asks us for help even though we're busy at work, or when a friend is surprised to hear us silently acquiesce to racial slurs, we have to be able to explain these choices to ourselves. This is what I mean by being clear-eyed about what we're

---

15. For recent work in the psychological literature on values affirmation, see Cohen et al., "Recursive Processes in Self-Affirmation"; Cohen and Sherman, "Psychology of Change"; Harackiewicz et al., "Closing the Social Class Achievement Gap."

doing—having an ethical narrative that we are able to articulate about which compromises we are willing and unwilling to make. Developing such a narrative allows us to knit together what we value in the various worlds we inhabit into a single, unified, and honest perspective.

4

Resisting Complicity

The path of upward mobility can exact painful ethical costs. A striver's earliest, most formative relationships can be undermined and threatened by the dynamics of moving up in a socioeconomically segregated and highly unequal society. As we saw in the last chapter, strivers may feel compelled to change in order to succeed, potentially in ways that jeopardize important aspects of their identities. This risk is particularly acute for those strivers who see their relationships with their families, friends, and community as central elements of their identities. Codeswitching offers a way for strivers to navigate those tensions. But codeswitching comes with its own dangers. A striver who is not thoughtful and reflective about what he or she values can end up behaving in ways that threaten his or her ethical integrity.

Accepting and adopting the norms that prevail in middle-class workplaces or educational institutions, even if only situationally, can further entrench those expectations, making it increasingly difficult for other strivers to break in. This means that strivers not only are liable to pay significant ethical costs for their success, but also through this success risk complicity in perpetuating the structural conditions that disadvantage other strivers like themselves and potentially entrench inequality and poverty in communities like their own.

The idea that honest and clear ethical reflection should be an integral part of upward mobility lies at the heart of this book. But such reflection inevitably takes us away from simply thinking about our own individual path and toward recognizing the ways in which we also uphold and embody the social structures that lead to ethical costs for other strivers and their communities. Strivers who succeed on the path of upward mobility find themselves moving from positions of relatively little power—student, child, job applicant, intern—to much more powerful ones—mentor, parent, employer, professional.[1] And whereas strivers who are starting out might feel quite constrained in their path by their socioeconomic position, family circumstances, or educational experiences, as they move up they increasingly gain power that can be used either to resist or to entrench the structures that largely determine the ethical costs that have been the focus of this book. We will now turn to considering how strivers might contend with the ethically difficult position they are in as a consequence of their success, bearing in mind that this is a recurrent challenge that strivers confront throughout their path.

The Tale of the Stairs

In Hristo Smirnensky's story "The Tale of the Stairs," a young working-class man strikes a bargain with the Devil.[2] He wants to climb a set of towering stairs in order to exact revenge on the nobles enjoying themselves at the top while the working class suffers in poverty down below. As he climbs the first steps, the Devil asks the young man for his hearing. When the young man agrees, the Devil replaces his ears so that the voices of moaning

---

1. For a very helpful take on these issues, see Zheng, "What Is My Role."
2. Smirnensky, "Tale of the Stairs." Thanks to Luc Bovens for directing me to this story.

from those down below are replaced by the sounds of laughter. As the young man races up the next steps, the Devil asks him for his vision. He agrees again, and the Devil replaces his eyes; now when the young man looks down, he sees healthy people in beautiful clothes. The final concessions the Devil exacts from the young man before allowing him to reach the top are his heart and his memories. These final replacements complete the transformation: the young man is now identical to the other people at the top, oblivious to the suffering below.

Smirnensky grew up in a poor Bulgarian family, died young of tuberculosis, and was never able to climb out of poverty despite finding some success as a poet. His short story is a dramatic allegory of the perils of upward mobility. To reach the top, the young man must transform, but what this transformation requires is losing everything that is essential to who he is. In short, he sells his soul. This story is an exaggeration, of course, but it points to the ways in which upward mobility changes those who undertake it. As the young man tragically illustrates, in the process one risks becoming complicit in the oppressive circumstances that made one's own path, and the path of other strivers, so challenging.

As we have seen, upwardly mobile students are confronted with competing pressures. One set stems from their relationships with their families and others in their home community. The other set arises as they become part of new communities—first, their school campus, and then, if all goes well, the professional world. In these new communities, opportunities are far more abundant; by becoming a part of them, endless possibilities appear within one's reach. But succeeding in this process of adaptation and acculturation can lead strivers to compound the price paid by those who stay behind. The toll is exacted first by the absence that the striver leaves behind and then again by the reinforcement of the barriers that, having overcome them, the striver is now in a position to perpetuate.

From Student to Professor

I too experienced this process of transformation in my path from student to college professor. One of my most vivid memories from my undergraduate education involves a class led by a well-respected philosopher notorious for subjecting his students to a "philosophical boot camp." It was a year-long course intended for serious philosophy students thinking about graduate school. The class started out with an enthusiastic 40 or so undergraduates; by the end, fewer than 8 of us remained. In one particularly keen memory, we weary survivors are sitting in a seminar room, and I am trying to answer a question as the professor looms over me, pounding the table. His exact words are lost to me, but his meaning is clear: "What is your point?! Make it already!" I can still feel the anxiety flooding every crevice of my body as I battle the tears threatening to embarrass me. I control my stammer and try my best to fake the confidence he expects. When I think about what I learned in college, I look back to that terrifying moment. Only a year later I would be in graduate school, confidently participating in advanced seminars and unwilling to back down when challenged. That undergraduate seminar certainly played a role in bolstering my confidence and—perhaps even more important—my ability to fake confidence when I lacked it.

Many years later, I became a professor myself, and with that position I gained much more power than I had as that frightened undergraduate. Yet when I first started teaching, I had little understanding of the ways in which I was playing a role in maintaining social structures that disadvantaged strivers. In graduate school, I received little instruction on how to teach and no guidance as to how to deal with class, gender, or racial dynamics in the classroom. When it came time for me to lead my own classes, I simply reenacted the teaching I had experienced as a student. I lectured and then would let those students who were already confident enough to raise their hands and make their voices heard monopolize the discussion. That's what was expected of me, and it was the easiest thing to do.

It was only when I started to reflect on my teaching and on the experiences my students were having that I began to see how in turning the class over to those students who were already confident in voicing their opinion, I had become complicit in perpetuating a college culture that privileges students who show up to college already knowing how to get the most out of it. Professors tend to notice the students who are vocal and participate. And these students are also the ones who feel comfortable going to office hours, arguing over a paper grade, or asking questions when they are confused. They get attention, and they also tend to get better grades and glowing letters of recommendation. A classroom environment that makes it easy for those students to shine will also tend to be one that feels unwelcoming to those strivers who feel out of place on a college campus. Let us return to my story of being a frightened undergraduate. The fact is that I made it as far as I did in that class in part because, notwithstanding the terror that this particular professor inspired in me, I myself was already the sort of student who participated in class discussion. I had learned to do so in my exclusive private school back in Peru. The intimidating nature of the "boot camp" atmosphere had already driven most of the timid and hesitant students away. And it is very likely that some of the students who were driven away were precisely those students who didn't feel at home in that kind of combative classroom environment—a thought that never occurred to my younger self. Rather, I felt proud that I had made it so far while others had not.

The benefits that stem from having the ability to confidently speak in front of a group of people or in response to an intimidating authority figure do not vanish at graduation. Among the handful of students who made it through that seminar with me, most of us did go on to graduate school, and, as far as I know, at least a third of us are professors. And in many career paths outside of academia, confidence and assertiveness are prized skills. So it is particularly important that those students who are liable to get "lost" in the halls of academia—particularly women, minorities, and first-generation students—learn to assert themselves, especially in interactions with those who are in positions of authority.

As a professor, I now find myself in a position to encourage those students who are liable to be overlooked. And now that I better understand the forces at play, I can make a concerted effort to live up to that responsibility in my classroom. For many of my students, what I ask of them is not easy. I can see that difficulty in the speed with which their heads tip down so that they can intently stare at their notebooks and avoid eye contact whenever I ask a question. Raja*, a student in my first-year writing seminar, was one of those for whom participation was challenging. An immigrant from South Asia, his written assignments demonstrated that behind his reluctant brown eyes was a bright and thoughtful mind eager to engage with the reading I had assigned. But every time I asked him to participate, his face would twist into a grimace. Surprisingly, a few weeks into the semester he came to office hours to try to convince me that he didn't need to talk in class. He said he would rather write than participate. There was a complicated mix of factors at play in his reluctance. Raja had a shy disposition, but, as he told me, he was also simply not used to expressing his opinion in this way. He had been taught to listen to the professor's ideas, not assert his own. I insisted that it was important that he practice speaking in front of his peers. Even as a doctor, which is what he aspired to be, it would be important for him to be able to speak to his colleagues. He looked at me glumly as I presented my arguments. As he left my office, he seemed unconvinced.

A few days later, he came into my office again to tell me that he had discussed our conversation with his older brother, who was also an immigrant to the United States. To Raja's surprise, his brother had agreed with me: in order to succeed in this country, Raja would have to learn to speak up. Raja and I devised a plan. He would come to class prepared to ask or say something and would raise his hand when he was ready. I would only call on him then. By the end of the term, Raja was contributing spontaneously, and the grimace on his face was gone.

What I was hoping to impart to Raja was a skill that my own undergraduate education had helped cement for me. On the surface, this seems like a success story: one of a student overcoming a deficit and developing a skill that would help him as he made his way through college and into his future career. But the truth is more complex. Raja's eventual willingness to speak up can also be seen as a story of acculturation—an immigrant kid being forced to reinvent himself to fit into the culture that dominates American educational institutions and middle-class workplaces. This culture places a premium on confidence, assertiveness, and being vocal—skills that, for some readers, will seem universally important and essential for success. And yet there are many communities in which these traits are not rewarded in the same way as they are in the middle-class, professional spaces Raja and I were seeking to enter; indeed, many other cultures prize deference to those who are older and more educated, listening rather than calling attention to oneself, and other community-based forms of interaction. As immigrants, Raja and I knew this. But I wanted to succeed as a philosopher in the Anglo-American institutions in which I was being educated; Raja wanted to succeed as a doctor in this country. And so we learned to do what was required.

But once strivers overcome these initial challenges and rise to positions of some power, they have to consider whether they are simply going to play a role in maintaining the social and cultural norms that presented a challenge for them or whether they can use their position to reform or subvert them. Now that I'm on the other side of the desk, I try to be explicit with my students about the dynamics at play even as I encourage them to participate, as I did with Raja, but I also endeavor to make sure that the students for whom this is a challenge do not slip through the cracks. And if Raja succeeds, I hope that he will reflect on how he can be a good doctor to strivers who might be too intimidated to ask him questions because he is in a position of authority over them. As we will see, this is the hard, reflective work of resisting complicity.

A Striver's Unique Position

As I have suggested, strivers who succeed find themselves in a position to reinforce the culture, norms, and social structures that led to the challenges they were trying to overcome in the first place. In chapter 2, we saw that socioeconomic segregation is one of the underlying structures that leads to the ethical costs of upward mobility. As an educated, middle-class professional, a successful striver can now buy into a neighborhood with a good school and make sure his or her children socialize with other middle-class children, thereby further entrenching neighborhood and social segregation along class lines.[3] We also saw in chapter 2 that the norms of middle-class workplaces and schools tend to favor an independent cultural model that prizes assertiveness and individuality. A successful striver is now in a position to hire that confident and vocal applicant who went to the "good" university, thereby continuing to confer advantages on those who have internalized the independent cultural model and enjoy easier access to those educational institutions. Finally, we saw that lack of access to social supports exacerbates ethical conflicts for strivers who are on the path of upward mobility. Our imagined successful striver is now in a position to impose on his or her students, employees, or colleagues inflexible, demanding schedules that make it harder for them to play caretaking roles at home.

These choices, while stemming from and reinforcing the striver's success, also have the potential to entrench the socioeconomic structures—housing, educational, and social segregation; cultural mismatch; lack of social supports—that exact painful ethical costs from strivers and their communities. More troublingly, strivers may forget about the challenges faced by people who grew up like them as they gain distance from those circumstances. Or they might internalize norms, as in the example we started with in this

---

3. For an insightful discussion of the obligations that parents have to promote social justice while fulfilling their duties as parents, see Brighouse and Swift, *Family Values*.

chapter, about being assertive or vocal that they then expect others to live up to. In all of these ways, it becomes easier to become complicit if one is unreflective.

I do not mean to imply that in making these choices individuals are to be blamed or chastised, although there is a very interesting philosophical debate about the extent of the individual obligations one incurs by virtue of the role that one plays in unjust social structures.[4] In many cases, we feel constrained by the expectations to which we are subject in our new positions as employers, professors, or colleagues. My point here is rather that we are all enmeshed in these structures. Though some of us benefit from this more than others, virtually all of us participate in a system that leads to disproportionate ethical costs for strivers, among other inequities. I do not aim to convince the skeptic who thinks we have no obligations to do what we can to advance a more just, fair society, but I do want to challenge the idea that a reflective striver can remain neutral with respect to these issues. To return to my own path as a professor, when I was unreflective about what was happening in my classroom, I unwittingly ended up favoring those students who were already well equipped for college, thus perpetuating their advantage. Until I did some more careful reflection, I had little understanding that replicating the teaching I had experienced was a form of entrenching a college culture that disadvantages strivers. But once I understood this, I could not simply go on as before. The social structures in which we live favor the status quo and thus benefit those who are already privileged; strivers who understand this cannot remain neutral and still view themselves as caring about justice.

This is not meant to deny that those who are born into privilege and continue to enjoy it have a greater responsibility to undermine the social structures that we discussed in chapter 2. To take one example among many: America's rampant residential segregation,

---

4. Philosopher Iris Marion Young is particularly compelling on this point; see her *Responsibility for Justice.*

via both class and race distinctions, is the product of decades of not only governmental policy, but also the choices made by individuals who have the resources to buy a home in a good school district and then vote for policies that exclude others who are less advantaged from enjoying the resources in their community. Similarly, and more germane to the central phenomena discussed in this book, administrators, professors, and upper-middle-class students are partially responsible for creating the atmosphere that makes some people of color and low-income students uncomfortable in college classrooms and, later, in offices and boardrooms. Shouldn't the onus be on the privileged—and I include myself here—to work to improve our institutions so as to accommodate those who are less advantaged? I agree wholeheartedly that it is critical that those who are most favored by the system take the obligations that stem from this privilege seriously, but this doesn't answer the question of what a striver can or should do.

Some individuals, by virtue of varying degrees of wealth, education, talent, or social connections, have a tremendous amount of power within our society. Others have little or no power because they lack many or all of these resources. Many of us fall somewhere in the middle. We have material resources, education, skills, or talent that we can use to make the world in which we live better. Although we can't donate billions of dollars, we can still make an impact.[5] The fact that those with tremendous amounts of privilege can do so much more does not absolve those who are less privileged from playing whatever small role they can. And strivers, by virtue of their unique position, have a distinct set of skills and

---

5. This paragraph touches on several tricky philosophical issues concerning how much we are all obligated to do for each other in an unjust society. For the purposes of this book, we only need accept the weaker claim that we all have some obligation. I don't intend to offer an argument about the extent of this obligation. For the classical argument in favor of a maximalist view of our moral obligations, see Singer, "Famine, Affluence, and Morality." For a view that being advantaged by injustice creates moral obligations, see Butt, "On Benefiting from Injustice."

knowledge that they can use to improve the lives of people growing up like they did.

First, strivers have knowledge that isn't easily available to those who haven't been born into disadvantage. They are more likely to understand the needs of underprivileged communities than is someone from a socioeconomically advantaged community. So many attempts at "helping" those who are disadvantaged go awry when ostensible solutions are conceived without true comprehension of the complexities of living in the communities at which they are aimed.[6] Second, successful strivers have gained valuable knowledge and skills through their education and professional experience and are uniquely positioned to develop solutions through diverse avenues, whether they be the law, economics, or urban planning. Finally, those who have made it into middle-class professions have acquired the skills needed to successfully navigate those communities and workplaces. Their capacity to codeswitch means that they are better able to advocate for disadvantaged communities because those in power are more likely to listen to them. In these ways, successful strivers have a unique and crucial role to play in the effort to create social structures that are fair and equitable. While those who have grown up with all of the advantages of being born to privileged positions have tremendous power and responsibility to make society more fair, strivers, by virtue of their unique skills and knowledge, have a critical role to play in guiding us toward a more just society that genuinely addresses the needs and concerns of disadvantaged communities.

Kimberly's Story: What to Do with a Harvard Degree?

I met Kimberly* on a sunny fall afternoon, sitting at a picnic table outside of the Harvard Business School, in which she was in the middle of a dual business and public policy master's program.

---

6. For an argument in favor of affirmative action that relies on a similar thought, see Anderson, "Fair Opportunity in Education." For a powerful description of such a gift gone awry, see Parker, "Gift."

Confident and thoughtful, her path to Harvard had started in a suburb of Cleveland. Her father had died when she was two. She had been raised by her mother and grandmother, an immigrant from Barbados. She told me that her family had, at times, relied on food stamps. Her shrewd grandmother, despite their financial struggles, had managed to buy a house in a middle-class neighborhood so that Kimberly could attend a good school; there, she was one of a few students who qualified for free lunch. In that middle-class school, she found a familiar kind of segregation: even though her school gradually enrolled more Black and Latino students, Kimberly was one of the few Black students in the high-achievement academic track. After graduating, she went to Ohio State on a full scholarship. And after working as a teacher for two years through Teach for America, and in management consulting for another two, she was now at Harvard, contemplating her next steps.

Kimberly's life trajectory was impressive. In many ways, her path embodied the ideal of the American education system—the transformation of a young, hardworking, and smart African American woman through public schooling. Her college degree, and soon her graduate degrees, would equip her with skills and knowledge that would make her valuable in many workplaces. But as we have learned, the trajectory out of poverty is rarely as straightforward as it first seems.

When I asked Kimberly whether she felt at home at Harvard, she considered the question carefully:

Yes and no. I can't participate as much because of money. Some of my friends just went to Napa, other people went to Iceland. People just go everywhere. I'll never be in that position. I don't think I feel out of place per se, but that's more because of my personality than anything else. I've talked to other students who have similar backgrounds that do feel more out of place, but they also kind of hide where they come from. I'm proud of where I come from. I deserve to be here just like anyone else. I think I deserve to be here more so. . . . I don't have a daddy to call and donate an extra wing of some building.

Kimberly had a very clear understanding of the barriers that she faced in her own life and, just as important, of the broad socio-economic factors that accounted for those barriers, both in her life and in the lives of many people like her. And, having been an educator, she was well aware of how those inequalities played out in what she saw around her at Harvard. But that awareness had become strength: it enabled her to feel proud about where she was and where she had come from, rather than embarrassed or uncomfortable.

Indeed, what was most remarkable about Kimberly was how clear she was about what she valued and what was important to her. She was clear about what her limits were; she knew what ethical trade-offs she was willing to make in order to succeed and, just as importantly, what she wasn't willing to change about herself. It pained her to have to say no when someone in her family asked her for financial help, but she was supporting herself through school. However, she tried to help her family as much as she was able to, financially and otherwise. When I asked her if the other students had different attitudes toward family, she said, with an unwavering expression on her face:

> Oh yeah, for sure. I think Americans in general are a lot more individualistic. I would never put my mother in a nursing home. She would live with me. She was living with me in Texas after she lost her job. It's not a question. You know, I've had friends try to say: "Oh, you don't have to do this." No, I don't think so. You take care of your family. That's number one. I wouldn't be where I am if my family didn't think that—if they didn't put all their money together and were house-poor so I could get an education.

Kimberly had done a remarkable job of staying connected to her family and community while learning how to navigate the world of the Ivy League. She had what I call a clear-eyed ethical narrative: a well-defined sense of what she valued and of what she was willing to sacrifice in her own trajectory; a deep understanding of how the trade-offs she had to make were embedded in larger, overarching socioeconomic structures; and a very clear sense of her own unique position within those structures and of her obligation to others who had also been born into disadvantage.

That Kimberly had a clear-eyed ethical narrative meant that she saw what was at stake in her situation and, just as importantly, the ways in which the challenges strivers like her faced were the result of socioeconomic conditions that needed to be changed. That gap—between the possibilities of her life and the lack of possibilities for the people she cared most about—posed a dilemma with which she was clearly struggling when we talked. She was keenly aware that others hadn't been as lucky as she had, but she seemed unsure of what she should do to help those who had been left behind. On the one hand, Kimberly wanted to go back to a community with people who had struggled like she had and "add real value" to their lives. But she also was worried about being able to take care of her family, telling me, "Fear of financial insecurity *is* real." She had observed that many of her peers, students from similar backgrounds, did not go back to their communities for the same reason: "They don't want to take the risk to do things because the things that will actually help their communities are a lot more risky than these jobs that just come to us and take us along and give us fat paychecks." Kimberly didn't wonder whether she should be concerned with the opportunities others lacked; rather, she was preoccupied with determining the best way to use her position to help them without jeopardizing her own hard-earned status.

Embracing Social Justice

Kimberley's dilemma is a deep and difficult one. For her book *Opting Out: Losing the Potential of America's Young Black Elite*, sociologist Maya Beasley interviewed Black students at Berkeley and Stanford. She found that these Black elite students did not aspire to enter the high-paying professions that many of their

White peers did. They were less likely to pursue careers in consulting, finance, technology, or engineering. Instead, they became social workers or teachers, or entered the nonprofit sector. Beasley highlights the many factors that were at play in the career choices of the Black students she interviewed, including their lack of exposure to these more lucrative career paths before college. But beyond these important influences on career path, she notes one additional factor that is crucial to the issue of the responsibilities of strivers—the sense of obligation that Black students like Kimberly feel to give back to their communities. She writes that the Black students she interviewed had "a strong orientation . . . toward community and social responsibility in their career interests. . . . Moreover, their perception of having been aided and encouraged along the way and the belief they have been privileged and blessed by persons and influences beyond their own talents provide a significant impetus to give back to their communities."[7] These students recognized that they were better off than most of the people with whom they had grown up, and their sense of obligation to their communities was profound.

We don't have to convince strivers that being upwardly mobile will put them in a position in which they can help others. Beasley's research supports what years of teaching strivers has suggested to me—many of these students are already abundantly, sometimes painfully, aware of the responsibility that comes from their hard-earned position. The difficulty, as we learned from Kimberly, is figuring out what to do next: *how* to embrace this responsibility and set about changing conditions that make it hard for others in their communities to access opportunities while *maintaining* their own hard-earned status.

The students whom Beasley interviewed show us one possible path forward: pursuing a career path in which one directly helps members of disadvantaged communities through social work or teaching. Social workers and teachers do crucial, important work,

7. Beasley, *Opting Out*, 142.

and a life spent in the service of others is certainly rewarding and valuable. But, as we saw in chapter 2, the challenges students face in the path of upward mobility stem from structural factors that individual social workers or teachers, no matter their dedication, will have a hard time changing. Of course, some strivers are uniquely suited to do the invaluable and crucial work of teaching and supporting those who are disadvantaged; there would be far fewer successful strivers if we didn't have talented and motivated teachers and social workers. But these are not the only ways to pursue social change.

Kimberly told me that she had left teaching because she felt that "the kids weren't getting what they needed to get, no matter how much I busted my ass, because I was only teaching them for one year and I had limited power." She thought that with an advanced degree, she could find a role crafting public policy in the education sector and gain more power to reform the structures that negatively affect others who have grown up like she did. When we met, she was still debating whether that was the best course of action, having been disappointed by several of her courses at the public policy school. She had found a more dynamic and inclusive environment at the business school; she was now considering whether what she had learned there could offer her a different way to help communities like those in which she had grown up.

In her book, Beasley suggests that teaching and other professions oriented toward helping others directly aren't the most effective path toward changing the systemic structures that lead to inequality. She thinks that the tendency of the young Black elite to pursue lower-paying professions is problematic. "Doing good" is important, but it isn't enough. She argues that the participation of the Black elite in Wall Street, K Street, and other places where political and economic power reside is just as important to "minimize economic risk, promote tolerance, and provide multiple lines of attack against racial injustice."[8] Consider, for example,

8. Beasley, *Opting Out*, 165.

the wealth gap between Black Americans and White Americans, which is stubbornly resistant to change even as the income gap closes.[9] Closing the wealth gap will require some Black students to go into very high-paying professions that allow their families to start amassing wealth and to find ways to garner political power to institute the kinds of changes to the tax system that might erode that gap. Still, as Smirnensky's "The Tale of the Stairs" warns us, this path is not without its dangers.

Joining the ranks of the elite isn't the only way to pursue structural changes or exercise political power. Voting, grassroots organizing, and myriad other forms of political engagement are powerful tools of social change. Across American history, from the civil rights movement to Black Lives Matter, we have seen the tremendous power of grassroots organizing. Nevertheless, I don't think we should underestimate the need to pursue structural changes from the inside.

Getting a college education, particularly at an elite university, can transform a student's life in many ways, but one of the most potent ones is the boost it provides to that student's economic, social, and political power within the society. This is why strivers are uniquely positioned to advance the interests of the communities from which they hail—they have gained power that others in their community lack. And, as we saw, there are many paths forward available to a talented striver who is serious about pursuing social justice. Some strivers have the skills, motivation, and knowledge that will make a teaching or social service career the most effective and satisfying path to pursue. Others are well equipped to participate in or lead social change movements. Still others are well positioned to join the ranks of the elite and use the power of those positions to push for structural change. In order to change the socioeconomic, cultural, and political conditions that so often privilege the interests of the better-off, we need to tackle the problem from a variety of positions within those structures.

9. For recent data on the wealth gap, see Wolff, "Household Wealth Trends."

Regardless of their chosen path, even the most well-meaning strivers are always combating the powerful forces involved in maintaining one's hard-earned status. For example, if during my first years at CCNY I had chosen to spend all of my time worrying about how to help my students and had neglected my research, I wouldn't have received tenure. Without tenure, I would have lost my teaching position and would not be able to help as many students. We can use the roles we have in society—teacher, lawyer, parent, community member—to help change social structures in ways that will make them more equal by engaging in what philosopher Robin Zheng calls "boundary-pushing."[10] However, maintaining those roles often requires that we work within those social structures in ways that tacitly endorse them. Consequently, even those strivers who take the responsibility of their unique position seriously must steer between two powerful forces that pull them in opposite directions—maintaining their hard-earned standing in a social structure that is often unjust and unequal and trying to reform that social structure to make it more just and equal.

Finding Time for Reflection

I have argued here that strivers are disproportionately saddled with painful ethical burdens. This is the plight of the student who is struggling in chemistry while at the same time feeling guilty about not rushing back home to help her sick sister. Strivers know that there is something fundamentally unjust about their situation. They frequently feel frustrated. But frustration isn't a comfortable resting place. To move beyond it, strivers must recognize that they are confronting symptoms that have an underlying cause. Thinking about justice and equality—that is, about how the world ought to be—provides strivers with the tools they need to articulate the nature of the injustice they face and to see it as a systemic problem rather than simply a personal challenge.

10. See Zheng, "What Is My Role," 878.

In previous chapters, I have argued that strivers need to consider the question of how to stay true to the people and values they care about while succeeding in the path of upward mobility. But as strivers come to recognize and reflect on the nature of the ethical costs they incur along this path, the deepening of that reflection process may lead them to consider broader questions. What would a more just and equitable society look like? And how can I use my unique set of skills, knowledge, and motivation to challenge current social structures so that they bring us closer to that ideal? Answering these questions is the work of a lifetime, and I am by no means suggesting that strivers will, or should, arrive at definitive answers. What I am suggesting is that understanding the nature of the ethical costs of upward mobility leads us to recognize the important role that social structures play in that process and our place within them.

The difficulty for strivers is not just that, by their nature, these questions are challenging, but that there is typically so little time or space for such individuals, who are already struggling against imposing odds, to engage in the kind of deep reflection required to adequately consider them.[11] Strivers' lives are often overburdened and hectic. I see this with my students. They struggle to study for exams, work, and care for their families and communities at the same time. The responsibilities they shoulder are heavy, so much so that I am sometimes astonished they are able to make it through college under such circumstances at all. Moreover, this difficulty is compounded by the current state of higher education: across college campuses, our pedagogical priorities for such students are changing. Philosophy, not to mention fields like literature, history, and sociology, are seen as valuable but unnecessary. Even though universities are uniquely suited to foster the critical tools that are essential for ethical reflection, many Americans are skeptical of what happens in universities and believe that an education at the sorts of institutions that strivers predominantly

---

11. The argument that follows is drawn from my "An Antidote to Injustice."

attend—community colleges and large public universities—should be focused on getting strivers into career tracks.[12] This shift stems in part from the fact that universities are capitulating to the devalorization of the humanities in public discourse, but also, and perhaps more significantly, from the fact that more students are attending college than ever before, and many of them are severely strapped for time and money. Each additional requirement costs those students dearly.

My university is an outlier and still requires students to take a wide array of liberal arts courses, including an introductory philosophy course, which I regularly teach. Every semester I encounter students who, understandably, are frustrated at having to spend their time and money reading Kant and Mill instead of focusing on classes that are directly related to their majors. It's all well and good, the thinking goes, for wealthy students who attend Harvard and Yale to indulge in pondering Dickens, Simone de Beauvoir, and W.E.B. Du Bois, but, as many of my students have asked me, why should strivers juggling a part-time job, a family, and a career-oriented degree take such courses? Though many come to appreciate what they learn in my class, it is undeniable that such a requirement can feel like another expensive and time-consuming hurdle in their path toward graduation.

As higher education increasingly focuses on teaching students what they need to know in order to perform a job in the world as they will find it, that vocational focus leaves little time to ask a central question: How *should* the world be? Engaging in this kind of reflection is not an indulgence, but a necessity. It is especially essential for those who are negatively impacted by the social structures that exist in the world we inhabit—the same people, sadly, who are the least likely to have access to the resources required for this kind of reflection.

12. See Pew Research Center, "Sharp Partisan Divisions" and "State of American Jobs."

The work of building a just society is imaginative. Yes, we need to be teachers, social workers, consultants, bankers, and grassroots organizers, but we also need to reflect on which ideals are guiding us as we try to harness those roles in the service of fostering a more just and fair world. All too often, the articulation of these ideals in public discourse is left to those who are already advantaged by the world as it exists.[13] Of course, these discussions are conducted over kitchen tables, at union meetings, and across campaign tables, but they rarely trickle up to the rooms where public policy is being crafted. If these ideals are going to be informed by the experience of those who are most impacted by injustice, we need strivers to be a part of these conversations as well. When universities that serve strivers narrow the focus of the education they offer to vocational training, they risk excluding them from these conversations.

My argument surely seems at least a little self-serving. It may not come as any great surprise that the philosopher thinks we should all study philosophy! But I am not arguing for a particular course or even a particular field. I don't advocate any one approach or methodology. I'm suggesting instead that undergraduate students be ensured the time, space, and framework within which to engage in deep reflection about their own values, as well as about justice, fairness, and what a better, more just world might look like. This might not even require studying philosophy; such reflection is possible in a sociology course, or maybe even in a club or a freshman seminar, though philosophers have spent thousands of years considering these questions. All colleges have the capacity, whether in their philosophy departments or elsewhere, to make reflection a priority sometime and somewhere within a student's education. And strivers, despite the many obligations they are already balancing, should take advantage of their college's offerings and engage in this kind of reflective work.

13. For an essential criticism of political theory and political philosophy on this score, see Mills, "Racial Liberalism."

My hope for instilling reflection at the heart of an undergraduate education is also a hope for my own field. Though philosophers are paid to think about the most important issues of life—and are supposed to help us see truths that are "universal" and thus applicable to all of us—my colleagues tend to come from a startlingly small segment of society. The field of philosophy tends to attract those who already have a privileged position in society: students who are wealthy, White, and male.[14] Many of the most elite universities with strong liberal arts programs also tend to be disproportionately White and wealthy.[15] Consequently, much of the philosophical dialogue concerning justice centers around work written by White, privileged men, even though this is the population that has the least to lose by maintaining the status quo. This is another reason why it is important for strivers to think through these questions. The intellectual and creative energy that will drive social change will come from those who have the most to gain from the system changing. Strivers are in a unique position to play this role.

14. American Academy of Arts & Sciences, "Racial/Ethnic Distribution of Degrees"; Pinsker, "Rich Kids Study English."
15. Chetty et al., "Mobility Report Cards."

5

Constructing an Ethical Narrative

The traditional narrative of upward mobility misrepresents the real ethical costs that strivers must pay to succeed. It portrays the sacrifices strivers make as a short-term investment of time, money, and effort that is handsomely repaid with the achievement of middle-class status. In this individualistic conception of upward mobility, social structures figure only as challenges to be overcome, rather than as social arrangements and institutions in which we all participate. Family, friends, and community are portrayed as allies or, if their support is not unwavering, obstacles rather than as individuals or entities that are themselves in need of support. Strivers who succeed have no reason to be ambivalent, because they are undoubtedly better off now than they were at the start of their journey. Those around them—family, friends, and community—should feel pride that one of their own made it.

I have argued that this narrative overlooks the ethical costs that strivers must bear and the ways in which those costs are also exacted on those with whom they have meaningful relationships. It also ignores the extent to which social structures—socioeconomic segregation, lack of a safety net, and cultural mismatch—concentrate these ethical costs in ways that disproportionately affect strivers and their communities. I have suggested that it is not unusual for strivers to struggle to balance the competing pressures they confront in their search for upward mobility. Success on this path often involves strivers changing in ways that distance them from what they find meaningful and valuable. These omissions fundamentally undermine the traditional narrative of upward mobility. As I will suggest in this chapter, we need a new, more honest narrative that can help strivers meet the inevitable ethical challenges they will face with a clear view of what is at stake. This clear-eyed ethical narrative is characterized by three central features: it is honest about the ethical trade-offs involved in striving, it clearly situates these choices in a specific socioeconomic and historical context, and it is ethical in that it encourages strivers to reflect on what is valuable and meaningful to them and on the impact they want to make on the world.

Carla: How Much Sacrifice Is a College Degree Worth?

Carla* was failing one of my classes. She was a philosophy major and had seemed engaged with the course for the first few weeks, despite often showing up late. But within a month, she was showing up less and less frequently, until finally I stopped expecting her in class. A couple of weeks before the end of the term, she appeared at office hours, ostensibly to find out whether there was anything she could do to salvage her grade. By that point in the semester, there was not; I was honest with her about this fact. Carla was disappointed but seemed to expect my response. In fact, unlike other students who have walked into my office in her situation, she didn't seem to want to plead for a passing grade or to convince me to accept late work. I think maybe she just wanted to let me know that her absence was not because she disliked the material or my teaching.

As we talked, it emerged that Carla was failing her other classes as well. The problem, she told me with a sigh, was that she had to work 50 to 60 hours a week at two jobs to support herself through college. Her parents refused to help her pay for her education, but they made too much to allow her to qualify for financial aid. She didn't want to take on loans. I felt helpless and upset. Carla appeared resigned.

Carla was neither the first nor, sadly, the last student in this situation to walk into my office. Most of my students at CCNY do qualify for financial aid, but it is rarely enough to cover their living expenses. Some have additional obligations, such as families to support or other financial responsibilities for which student aid does not account. So they work.[1] And the more they work, the less time they have to devote to their courses. Many of these students fall behind, fail classes, or fail to complete requirements. A substantial number drop out. In fact, William Bowen and Michael McPherson have argued that one of the biggest challenges facing higher education right now is low college completion rates, particularly at institutions that serve strivers, such as my own.[2]

But what incensed me was that Carla blamed herself for not being able to work full-time, take a full load of courses, and do well. I told her that virtually anyone in her situation would end up in the same position. No one has enough time to devote to his or her studies while working that many hours. But, she insisted, you hear about people who do it all the time—support families, work full-time, and graduate from college. Of course, such extraordinary people do exist. I have met a few of them. And, honestly, I do not know how they do it. But why should this be expected of all strivers? Why should that kind of all-consuming sacrifice be the price that the disadvantaged have to pay in order to earn a college degree? And why should we think that failure in the face of such obstacles reflects an individual's unwillingness to work hard?

Carla's dilemma illustrates some of the shortcomings that undermine the traditional narrative surrounding higher education.

1. Goldrick-Rab, *Paying the Price*, is essential reading on this point.
2. Bowen and McPherson, *Lesson Plan*.

Not only is a college degree portrayed as worth any cost—whether financial, ethical, or both—but students are expected to make herculean efforts to achieve it. This narrative had not only sunk Carla's semester (and tuition money), but fundamentally undermined her self-confidence. She assumed that she simply had not worked hard enough.

As I overcame my anger, Carla and I started talking about what a realistic path would be for her to get her college degree. We determined it would probably take her a long time to reach a position in which she could fully devote herself to her classes. She would have to make many sacrifices in the interim and negotiate tense family dynamics surrounding her choices. "So is it worth it?" she asked. I couldn't provide a straightforward answer to that question, because, as I hope it has become clear in the course of this book, I do not think that anybody but Carla can determine the right answer. Instead, Carla and I discussed why she wanted to get a college degree, the sacrifices she would have to make to succeed, how certain unjust aspects of the higher education system were hampering her ability to pursue that degree, and how having (or not having) that degree would impact her future. In other words, we started building the elements of what I will describe in this chapter—a clear-eyed ethical narrative.

Though our conversation did not yield a clear answer to her question that afternoon, Carla still thanked me profusely for speaking to her. Nobody, she told me, had been so open and honest with her about what was at stake. Deciding whether or not to pursue a degree would be part of a lengthy, evolving process, one that only she could undertake herself. Similarly, I don't expect this book to deliver definitive answers to the strivers who read it. That is the nature of ethics and of living a reflective and ethical life. The language of ethics helps us organize our experiences and understand the nature of the problems we confront. But while recognizing and reflecting on what we value enriches and deepens our understanding of ourselves and of our world, it does not lead to simple answers. The problem with the traditional narrative of upward mobility is that it obscures the most challenging aspects of this process and offers an inadequate and facile blueprint that many accept as universal.

In this chapter we discuss how to craft an honest, alternative narrative of upward mobility. This narrative provides not answers, but rather a framework that can help strivers confront the questions they will face in a reflective way. Such an approach involves putting together all of the elements we have discussed thus far: recognizing those aspects of one's life that are valuable and meaningful but might be undermined in the process of moving up, situating those costs in the proper socioeconomic context in a way that recognizes the extent to which they disproportionately burden strivers, navigating the competing pressures on one's identity that upward mobility creates, and resisting one's complicity in a society that is unfairly structured so as to compound the hurdles already faced by those who are most disadvantaged.

The Elements of the Ethical Narrative

We are creatures who enjoy stories. We are enthralled by stories of others, certainly, but just as critically, throughout history and across cultures, we have been driven to construct our own.[3] Stories help us organize our lives by extracting meaning from the messy reality of the moments that make up everyday experience. A narrative can help us articulate what we value and, crucially, where we are headed. Social psychologists have found that the narratives we employ can be powerful motivators but can also constrain us.[4]

It is no surprise that most of us prefer to hear narratives that inspire us. Consider the story of Sonia Sotomayor—raised in the

3. This hermeneutic approach to the self can be seen in philosophy; see MacIntyre, *After Virtue*; Taylor, *Sources of the Self*. More naturalistic versions of this approach can be found in Dennett, "Self as a Center"; Schechtman, *Constitutive of Selves*.

4. For the importance of such narratives to the performance of college students, see Wilson, Damiani, and Shelton, "Improving the Academic Performance"; Stephens, Hamedani, and Destin, "Closing the Social-Class Achievement Gap."

Bronx by her widowed mother, she managed to earn a spot at Princeton, and then Yale, and ended up with a seat on the highest court in America.[5] These up-by-one's-own-bootstraps narratives offer powerful motivation, encouraging us to believe that such feats are also possible for the rest of us if we are willing to work hard and persevere. But, as we have seen again and again, such narratives obscure the reality of upward mobility.

The evidence of that reality is abundant, even if we don't want to see it. Upward mobility is not the norm for those born into low-income families in the United States.[6] Still, Americans on the whole vastly overestimate how much upward mobility actually occurs in our country.[7] Furthermore, as I have argued in this book, for many students the process of upward mobility requires far more than perseverance: it also requires brutal decisions and painful sacrifices, threatens their relationships with those who matter most to them, and destabilizes their sense of identity and belonging. The story of upward mobility isn't just one of gains; it is also one of losses. Narratives of upward mobility tend to flatten crucial differences in the challenges that various groups of people experience depending on their place in society. And, most problematically, they tend to portray upward mobility as the solution to a range of problems—from poverty to segregation to lack of opportunity—while ignoring the ways in which the barriers for low-income communities remain unchanged even as a select few make it.

But using evidence and statistics from the social sciences to call into question the validity of the traditional narrative of upward mobility only takes us so far. Simply pointing out the inaccuracies of this story will not suffice to eliminate it. Stories can captivate us regardless of their accuracy. Thus, what we need is an alternative narrative of upward mobility that can displace the traditional

---

5. Her autobiography is inspiring and beautifully written; see Sotomayor, *My Beloved World.*

6. See Chetty et al., "Is the United States."

7. See Kraus and Tan, "Americans Overestimate Social Class Mobility."

narrative, one that is both uplifting and honest. I grew up with such a narrative—that of the immigrant striver. Immigrant strivers are those, like myself, who are seeking opportunities for a better life through immigration. Of course, this narrative, like all stories, is vulnerable to distortion, but it is more honest in some crucial ways than the typical story of upward mobility that we tell. Specifically, the immigrant striver's narrative is upfront about the character of the sacrifices that are required—the ethical costs are front and center. I want to be clear that in what follows I'm relying on an idealized version of the immigrant striver's story; it is all too easy to paint the immigrant story with an overly broad brush that obscures all subtlety from an individual's experience. My hope is that the simplifications will help to highlight some of what is missing from the typical tale we offer strivers who are not immigrants.

Consider the immigrant who, faced with a corrupt, autocratic regime that has stifled opportunities for economic advancement in her home country, has to find those opportunities elsewhere. She packs up her bags and leaves her family, friends, and community to go to another country with better prospects. She cries almost every night during her first few months in this new country, missing everything about home terribly. She is forced to take any job she can find no matter how little it pays or how badly she is treated in order to save money so that she can open her own business, go to college, or put herself in a position to find a better job. She must deal with abusive employers, not to mention unwelcoming neighbors; she has to learn to live with all manner of small slights and racial stereotypes. But she adapts. She learns the language, the culture, and how to navigate new social relationships. She makes friends. Whenever she has a little extra money, she sends it back home to help her mother and the rest of the family she left behind.

Throughout these trials she has a story she can tell herself—one that motivates her to push forward while allowing her to reflect on the costs of doing so. She is sacrificing many aspects of her life that she has valued—her relationships back home, proximity to family and community, immersion in her own culture—in order to make a better life for herself. She recognizes that she is making these trade-offs in the service of goals she values. Understanding that the demands of her path to upward mobility may jeopardize things that matter to her can lead her to seek ways to mitigate those losses—whether by finding a community with ties to the one she left behind or by making sure to stay in touch with those back home whenever she can. If she has a certain level of education, she might also situate her circumstances in global economic and political conditions, all of which combine to negatively impact people who grow up in situations like hers. After she gains some success, she, like many immigrants, might reflect on her new position and think about how she can help those who stayed behind or other immigrants in her community who are struggling. Of course, each immigrant crafts his or her own unique narrative—some might be less reflective, others will involve fewer trade-offs, and most will evolve over time.

I grew up with an immigrant striver narrative because, quite frankly, it was the story of my family. My grandmother had emigrated from Arequipa, a city in the Andes, to Lima, the larger and wealthier capital of Peru; my mother and aunt emigrated from Peru to Europe; and I, too, was expected to also find opportunities elsewhere. Before embarking on that journey, however, I had already had my eyes opened by this immigrant narrative to the potential costs (and gains) of this path. When I got to college, my family, like that of many first-generation college students, couldn't help me figure out what to look for in an advisor, what classes to sign up for, or how to become a part of the campus community. But luckily, they had prepared me to be an immigrant—that is, to expect to feel lonely, distant, and out of place. I had seen my mother and my aunt overcome that initial displacement in Europe and build a community and home for themselves abroad. In some sense, this gave me an edge when I got to college. While, like most other first-year students at Princeton, I often worried that I didn't belong or had been admitted by mistake, I could attribute some of my discomfort to being an immigrant. My understanding of myself as an immigrant also helped me find a community at Princeton. My friends were not themselves immigrants, but many of them were the children of immigrants. In retrospect, I realize that I was drawn to them because they understood the cultural straddling I was undertaking. They also had experience with straddling the culture they grew up with at home and that of school and the world outside of home. The narrative of the immigrant striver allows those of us who are immigrants to weather some of the feelings of alienation and displacement that form a part of our trajectory and, if all goes well, to find a community in which we can feel comfortable negotiating those cultural differences.

Certainly, we should be wary of simply transferring this immigrant narrative to the distinctive experience of strivers who are not immigrants, but it is valuable to reflect on it all the same. The immigrant narrative is built on four distinct features that I think, not coincidentally, are also the crucial elements of an ethical narrative. First, it affirms a plurality of ethical goods that matter to one's life—one's relationships, culture, and connection to one's community—rather than focusing only on educational or economic achievement. Second, it makes it clear that some of those ethical goods will have to be traded off or sacrificed for the sake of other goods and opportunities. Ideally, though not always, it situates these trade-offs in a historical, political, and socioeconomic context. Third, it is cognizant of the risks to one's identity that the process of immigration entails. As the immigrant striver becomes more at ease navigating the new country, his or her skill at navigating the culture of the home country may wane. And finally, though this is not as frequently a part of the immigrant narrative as I think it ought to be, the experience of being an immigrant enables one to think more critically and reflectively about the broader social, political, and economic context of both one's adopted country and one's home, and how one might play a role in changing them for the better. In what follows, I tease out each of these features in more depth.

RECOGNIZING ETHICAL GOODS

In the traditional narrative of upward mobility, strivers sacrifice effort, time, money, and, in some depictions, fun. Writing about his childhood in Indonesia, Barack Obama describes his mother waking him up at four in the morning to study for three hours before school because she worried that the school he was attending wasn't rigorous enough.[8] This scenario embodies the image of upward mobility that many of us hold: the striver is the person who gets up at the crack of dawn to study instead of getting a little bit more sleep, the person who stays at the library until it closes instead of going to a party. But, as I argued in chapter 1, that image is inevitably oversimplified. Yes, strivers work hard. But such efforts are nearly always accompanied by other valuable and meaningful sacrifices that are just as important, though rarely discussed.

In order to recognize the ethical goods that strivers are at risk of sacrificing, we need the language of value. I am not suggesting that we talk about our "values" in the abstract. As we saw in the first chapter, many of the ethical goods at stake for strivers are particular. So the questions strivers need to consider should focus on the particular relationships and communities that make their lives meaningful and valuable. Who are the people who matter to you? How do these people figure in your life? What parts of these relationships do you value? What aspects of these relationships are difficult? Similarly, it is easy to state broadly that we value our culture. It is both more difficult and much more worthwhile to identify the particular aspects of our culture that we value. Are there aspects of your culture that you reject? Why? Instead of talking about the value of friendship or community, tell me about your friends and your community. How, specifically, do they contribute to your life, and how do you contribute to theirs? Reflecting on these questions can allow us to more clearly recognize and

8. Obama, *Dreams from My Father*, 47–48.

deliberately affirm the value in our lives and the many people and relationships that embody that value.

There is substantial evidence that "values affirmation" interventions can boost the academic achievement of minority students. In these exercises, students are asked to write about what they value and why they value it. As one set of researchers notes, "A key aspect of the affirmation intervention is that its content is self-generated and tailored to tap into each person's valued identity."[9] They point to a study that finds that asking a group of seventh graders to reflect on a value that is important to them—relationships with friends, family, or musical or artistic interests—can significantly boost the grade point average of minority students even up to two years after the exercise.[10] Psychologists think that self-affirmation exercises work by countering the effects of perceived threats to a student's self-image that arise in challenging environments. By broadening the students' perspective beyond the threat in front of them, students are able to regain a sense of self.

This notion that recognizing and acknowledging the relationships and pursuits that we value can give us the perspective we need to keep us motivated when we confront difficulties and setbacks is quite compelling. But I believe that strivers in particular need values affirmation for another reason as well—to build narratives that can help them navigate the ethical challenges of upward mobility. We need to recognize the ethical goods at stake in order to be honest about the true costs of striving. Unfortunately, our traditional narrative of upward mobility fails to acknowledge the value and necessity of such reflection. Rather than highlight the plurality of goods at stake, this narrative reduces the complexity and interconnectedness of an individual's life to the goal of individual educational and economic achievement. Rather than helping students appreciate what is valuable in their lives right now,

---

9. Cohen and Sherman, "Psychology of Change," 337.

10. See Cohen and Garcia, "'I Am Us'"; Cohen et al., "Recursive Processes in Self-Affirmation."

the traditional blueprint suggests that the striver must cultivate a narrow focus on an uncertain and distant future "success."

Yet we are trading off some ethical goods for the sake of other ethical goods. It is just as crucial that strivers identify what they seek to gain beyond financial security and a good job. What are those ethical goods that we are aiming to achieve? Why does a college degree matter in their pursuit? Why are all these sacrifices worth it? The answers to these questions at times seem obvious to those of us who have earned college degrees, but they are by no means obvious to all students on this path. When I've discussed these issues with my own students, I'm surprised by how infrequently they have been given opportunities to reflect on their own education. Few really understand what they are supposed to be getting out of their classes, why certain classes are required, and what the ultimate value of their education might be. However, given this opportunity to reflect on their education, I find that my students have very thoughtful and engaged discussions about the value of a liberal arts education, the utility of a vocational path, and whether they are learning anything useful in their time at college. Many of them tell me that despite the fact that they're spending significant amounts of time, money, and effort getting into and making it through college, they've rarely, if ever, engaged in these conversations with each other, their parents, or their professors.

This type of discussion is, in fact, a critical step in understanding the ethical trade-offs at stake in the path toward upward mobility. Without it, how can strivers understand what they are making these huge sacrifices to achieve? If they are giving up goods that are meaningful and valuable to them now, what do they stand to gain that will make their lives meaningful and valuable in the future? Of course, a college degree offers a clearer path toward a good job and economic security. But students also need to be able to see the intrinsic value that their education affords them beyond the credential. This requires that they ask themselves: Am I becoming a better person, a more informed citizen, or a more productive member of society through what I am learning? If so, how? The answers to these questions may evolve over time as an individual's perspective matures, but reflecting on them provides strivers with an opportunity to broaden their understanding of why they are in college as they confront the difficult challenges that we have been discussing in this book thus far.

One of the aspects of the immigrant narrative that is so compelling is the feeling, shared by many immigrants, of pride in one's country and culture. Even as we try to enter a new country with a new culture, we do not feel compelled to diminish or devalue what we left behind. This is, in part, why many immigrants were deeply offended when President Donald Trump called the places from which they came "shithole countries."[11] Leaving one's country is frequently a great sacrifice because what is left behind, whatever problems might reside there, is still something that is loved and cherished. Trump did not confine his offensive rhetoric to the immigrant context. He called inner-city Chicago a "disaster" and referred to it as a war zone comparable to Afghanistan.[12] His language was widely condemned, but Trump's hurtful bluster tapped into an image that remains alive and well in the popular imagination. The places that strivers transcend are often portrayed as places that are better left behind—the ghetto, the inner city, the impoverished rural village. Any hint of longing for what came before is often met with confusion. But, as we have seen, that notion of a place that is better left behind is overly simple and misleading. Frequently, meaningful and valuable aspects of strivers' lives continue to reside there—no matter how impoverished those communities may be—and turning one's back on them for the sake of better economic opportunities and a good life, while possibly necessary, is not therefore easy. Recognizing that complexity by acknowledging the value in what we have left behind is the first step in building an honest ethical narrative.

11. Dawsey, "Trump Derides Protections for Immigrants."
12. Rumore, "Trump on Chicago."

SITUATING ETHICAL COSTS

Clearly identifying the ethical trade-offs at stake in the path toward upward mobility lays the groundwork for the next step in constructing an ethical narrative—situating those trade-offs in a historical, political, and socioeconomic context. The traditional story of upward mobility misrepresents this path in a variety of ways, notably by shifting our focus almost entirely to the individual and his or her noble struggle upward while ignoring how that individual is embedded in a community defined by relationships and, more broadly, by social, political, and economic structures. In order to truly understand the situation that strivers confront, we must trace the connection between the ethical costs they incur and the social and economic structures on which those costs depend. Strivers need to know that the reason they seek opportunities outside of their communities is rarely because these communities are deviant or because the culture that strivers bring into the classroom is lesser. They must recognize that our society has structured access to such opportunities in ways that make it that much harder for them to succeed. Failing to acknowledge this is not only dishonest, but also demeaning and disempowering to these students.

The life stories of Sonia Sotomayor and Steve Jobs, despite the vast differences between these two notable figures, amount to essentially the same uplifting story when abstracted through the lens of the traditional upward mobility narrative. They both worked hard and transformed their lives. You can do it too, the implication goes. The misrepresentation is in the suggestion not that those at the bottom can move upward—of course, some do—but that the individual, simply by dint of hard work and effort, can transcend the vast social, political, and economic forces that structure the opportunities and challenges that confront us. We only need to dig a little deeper to see that in almost all stories of upward mobility, structural forces have conspired to make an individual's success more or less likely. For instance, Steve Jobs's parents, when they noticed their adopted child was gifted, were able to buy a house in a better school district so that Jobs could get a top-notch education and, crucially, gain exposure to a lot of the earliest advances in technology that would provide a stepping stone to his career. Jobs certainly took a risk by dropping out of college, but he already had amassed considerable technological skills that enabled him to land a job at Atari soon after.[13]

To dig deeper, a striver must ask him- or herself: Are there economic, social, or other structural factors that might be at play in this difficult situation I'm confronting? How can I better understand those factors and their impact on my path? What can I learn about the community I'm joining and the community I come from? What sorts of barriers am I likely to encounter because of my class, race, or gender?

Strivers who understand the role that factors such as residential segregation or lack of healthcare access play in their position in society also understand that many of the challenges they confront and the ethical costs they will have to bear stem not from their abilities or skills but rather from the situation into which they were born. With this knowledge, a striver is able to conceive of his or her experience in a way that he or she wasn't able to before. But the resulting insight is by no means comfortable. Understanding that the family into which you were born, the neighborhood in which you grew up, or the school that you attend play such critical roles in your path can make you feel reduced to a mere statistic, devoid of agency.

Upon reading about the experiences of first-generation college students, I also have felt dispirited at seeing my feelings of ambivalence and unease so clearly accounted for by my family background. And I have seen that same uncomfortable realization descend upon my students. In my Philosophy of Race course, we combine philosophical analysis with social science. For the students, most of whom are racial minorities, it can be difficult to read about the statistics concerning racial discrimination in

13. Isaacson, *Steve Jobs.*

employment.[14] They cannot help but ask themselves how many times their résumés have been overlooked because their name sounds Latino or Black. But reflecting on this issue from an ethical perspective forces us to do more than simply resign ourselves to our social position, no matter how challenging that might be.

There are aspects of our lives that matter to us deeply, and in order to do right by them, we must affirm our agency within the constraints we face. We must decide whether to attend class or work extra hours to support our family. Understanding that this decision is not one faced by every college student and that it stems from unfair inequalities in access to certain resources helps contextualize the choices we make. But understanding that doesn't dissolve the decision or its consequences for one's education or the people one loves. Understanding the context helps us see the decision more clearly for what it is—a constrained choice—but it is not meant to decide the question either way.

One of my students told me that when he came to college, he thought he would learn about a different world. Instead, he found himself getting angry when the focus in some of his classes kept turning back to his own community in the inner city, which was marred by poverty, violence, and lack of opportunity. He didn't dispute what his professors said, but he was upset that they saw his world as something to be studied. Yet as he approached graduation, he came to appreciate the broader perspective that he had gained and the reflection about his own community that it had sparked. It is this subsequent reflection that can allow strivers to move past the initial difficulty of seeing their lives as something to be studied and craft a reflective narrative for themselves.

When I was young, my grandmother was adamant that opportunities for advancement were to be found elsewhere, because life in Lima in the 1980s was marred by terrorism, hyperinflation, and a stagnant economy. I had seen how hard it had been for my mom

14. The classic paper on this is Bertrand and Mullainathan, "Are Emily and Greg More Employable Than Lakisha and Jamal?"

and aunt to immigrate to Europe, but I was also aware of how privileged I had been relative to other children in Peru by virtue of the sacrifices my family had made and very good luck. As I learned more in school about the history of colonialism and the influence of the United States in Latin America, I also came to appreciate the ways in which the lack of opportunities in our country was tied to a broader set of geopolitical incentives and policies that unfairly disadvantage those born in the global south. This understanding helped me contextualize what I saw around me and, later, what I saw when I arrived in the United States. I was entering a world that hadn't been designed for people like me. This thought can be deflating, but, as we will see, it can also be empowering.

NAVIGATING AN EVOLVING IDENTITY

Our relationships and communities shape who we are and how we think of ourselves. When those aspects of our life are threatened, parts of our identity are also under threat. In chapter 3, we discussed cultural codeswitching as a way of trying to curb such threats. Strivers codeswitch in order to effectively inhabit two worlds—the one they are coming from and the one they are entering—by changing how they act and behave depending on the context. I argued that codeswitching cannot be used to avoid the ethical costs of upward mobility because of the conflicts that inevitably arise as overlapping demands from the different spheres that the codeswitcher inhabits come into competition with one another. Our selves are not divided. While it is possible to inhabit different worlds in different ways at different times, it is virtually certain that a moment will arrive when we must choose where we stand. An ethical narrative can guide us in making such a choice.

After we have recognized the ethical costs of our path and situated them in a larger historical, political, and socioeconomic context, we must determine through reflection what goods we are willing and unwilling to sacrifice. This process of determination is the next step in the development of an ethical narrative. The striver who is torn between wanting to fulfill familial obligations and remain close to his or her home community while also feeling driven to change in ways that would make it easier to succeed in his or her chosen path faces a conflict. Being buffeted between these two pressures can leave strivers unmoored, unsure of who they are. To respond to the conflict reflectively, strivers must recognize what is central and important to them. If being a dutiful child and a good college student really matter to them, they have to determine how much they are willing to sacrifice when these domains of life come into competition.

Every college student has to negotiate a changing identity while at college. Education, by its nature, changes us in profound ways. But the transformation of a well-off student with college-educated parents need not involve a radical refashioning of the self that puts the student in conflict with his or her family or community. Though such a student might change in ways that are dramatic, and some do end up in conflict with their family or community, this transformation is generally not a response to a tension that is inherent in the distance between his or her home community and the college community. For many strivers, responding to these competing pressures on their identity is a central part of the college experience.

As part of constructing an ethical narrative, strivers must consider questions such as: How much of what matters to me am I willing to sacrifice in order to succeed? To what extent am I prepared to change? How will I resist the pressure to change in ways that are in tension with these things that matter to me? What do I need to do to maintain my relationships with those I care about? Reflecting on these questions is a difficult and highly personal undertaking. The process is not static. At different points in time, the things that matter most to strivers might change. Their existing relationships may evolve, they may develop new relationships and interests, or they may start to feel more comfortable in their new community in ways that will change their sense of who they are.

Here I think we can also learn a lot from the immigrant narrative, which is upfront not only about the potential ethical costs and trade-offs inherent to the immigrant's journey, but also about the threats to one's identity that often accompany these costs. Many immigrants feel torn between two communities to which they feel equally connected. My grandmother immigrated to the capital as a young woman and has lived there ever since, but even though decades passed before she went back to visit the mountain town of her birth, she still considers herself *Arequipeña*. Though it is Lima she misses when she goes abroad, she still worries herself sick over what is happening to nieces back in Arequipa whom she has barely seen. This extended family still calls her frequently, over 60 years after she left, and makes constant requests for financial and emotional support. Her daughters, my mother and my aunt, cannot quite understand why, even in her old age, she insists on dutifully sending clothes and money back to her extended family. She rebuffs the suggestion that this burden is too much for an old lady like her. Her family in Arequipa is important to her, of course, but these gifts and calls are also how she stays connected to where she came from and to an identity she still holds dear.

Many immigrants understand that moving to a new country potentially threatens their connection to the places from which they hail, and that the loss of this connection might change them. Strivers who are aware that upward mobility poses a similar threat are better able to navigate the potential effect on their values and identity in a reflective and thoughtful way.

RESISTING COMPLICITY

Recognizing the ethical costs at stake in upward mobility and situating them in the context of social and economic structures requires that the striver critically evaluate his or her own position in society. This reflective process explicitly positions seemingly personal choices within a much broader social perspective, forming the groundwork for the next step in the construction of an ethical narrative. It is at this point that strivers must acknowledge that upward mobility puts them in an ethically fraught position.

As they rise to positions of greater power, it is easy to become complicit in the socioeconomic structures that broadly make it difficult for strivers to succeed. And if, like many strivers, they want to reform these structures and erode the obstacles that strivers face, they must think very carefully about how to do so. They must reflect on the ways in which they are implicated in those social structures without losing their hard-won position. This must be understood as an evolving and iterative process of reflection, a long-term undertaking that requires continuous adjustment and reconsideration as the striver advances through college and beyond. An ethical narrative should help the striver think not only about the challenges and sacrifices that will have to be made on the path of upward mobility, but also about the potential impact he or she can have at various points along that path.

As a first-generation college student, it can be hard to see yourself as having the agency and power to change social structures, making the construction of an ethical narrative all the more important. One of the most enjoyable classes I occasionally teach is a small first-year seminar that is meant to be a writing-intensive introduction to college that helps foster small cohorts of students who are new to CCNY. These students are encouraged to take other classes with each other with the hope that they will develop bonds within their smaller group and form learning communities. Evidence suggests that such groups increase college retention.[15] This course is also an opportunity for students to work closely with a college professor, and we are encouraged to talk to students about strategies for college success. Sometimes when I teach this class, I will recruit one of my previous students, now a sophomore or junior, to speak to the class about how to make it through college. After only an additional year or two at CCNY, these students are already in a position to help other strivers. And as students move through college and into the professional world, there are ever more ways they can do their part to make the world a more

15. See Tinto, "Taking Retention Seriously."

just place. My work, this book, was born out of that desire. My power is limited, but it is not nonexistent. And this is the realization that the ethical narrative spurs.

In this regard, the immigrant narrative is perhaps more limited than we would ideally like it to be. While it does urge the immigrant striver to think about the responsibility that comes with succeeding, this obligation is often narrowly focused on family and perhaps compatriots, rather than on changing social and economic structures that lead to the global inequalities that spur immigration in the first place. Many immigrants go abroad to seek economic opportunities so that they can provide financial support to those who stay behind, and the money that immigrants remit is often a vital boost to the livelihood of the developing world.[16] But these financial flows fail to significantly reform the structural factors involved in creating and maintaining global inequality. Consequently, though the scale of remittances can be seen as a sign of how seriously immigrants treat the obligations that stem from their success, from a broader perspective these transfers are insufficient.

Some of the most popular contemporary stories of upward mobility in the United States do better on this score than the immigrant narrative. Barack Obama and Sonia Sotomayor are quite clear in their memoirs that their path was deeply shaped by a desire to go into public service. But, as I argue in chapter 4, there are many ways to challenge the unjust social structures that shape our lives. Doing so requires ongoing reflection on some of the following questions: What challenges does my community, and do I as part of that community, experience in striving for a better life? How might I best use the skills and knowledge I have gained to make our society more just and mitigate some of those challenges for others who were also born into disadvantage? In what ways do I unwittingly reinforce those social structures that I think are unjust or unfair? To answer these questions, strivers (and the rest of us) must think more deeply about the features that would define a

---

16. United Nations, "Sharp Increase in Money."

more just society. This ongoing process of reflection is demanding, but I think it is crucial if we are to move beyond the individualistic assumptions underlying the traditional story of upward mobility.

Constructing an Ethical Narrative Together

In this book I have argued that we need a new narrative of upward mobility. I have discussed the elements of these narratives and their importance. But how and where are these narratives constructed? I believe that we construct such narratives by engaging in the kind of reflection prompted by listening to each other's stories. As strivers and first-generation college students, we need to hear the honest, painful, and often-messy stories of the paths taken by others like us. We need to recognize the possibility embedded in our own stories in the stories of others. This recognition can prompt us to take on the work of crafting narratives of our own.

As I have stressed throughout this chapter, the construction of an ethical narrative is a reflective, ongoing, and highly personal process, something that each striver must do on his or her own. But there is much that educational institutions, particularly colleges and universities, can do to facilitate the development of these narratives. It is beyond the scope of this book to suggest a curriculum or provide pedagogical instructions about how to do so. However, I do want to highlight two points that I think all of us who care about strivers and their success in higher education must keep in mind.

First, we should note that one of the best ways for strivers to understand the true costs of upward mobility is to learn from others who have experienced these costs firsthand. Experience is a powerful teacher. As a result, educational institutions should seek out more first-generation college graduates to serve as professors, graduate students, and administrators.[17] At the same time, it

---

17. Lisa Delpit, a leading theorist of education, has argued that we need more teachers of color in K–12 education precisely because those teachers have cultural and experiential knowledge that is important to teaching. See her *Other People's Children*.

is critical that these institutions foster cultures that enable these first-generation graduates to share their stories. This doesn't mean that professors need to bare their lives to their students or that classrooms should be places where people merely sit around and share life experiences (though this is a frequent mischaracterization of what "culturally congruent" or "diverse" education looks like). But it does require that professors know how to create an inclusive classroom environment.

When my students find out that I'm also a first-generation college student, I can see them relax a little bit and open up in the classroom. This matters to their educational experience. Let me offer one recent example. A colleague of mine was concerned about one of her students; he was very quiet and hardly said anything during classroom discussions but had written an exceptional paper that she worried he had plagiarized. My colleague is a very good teacher, one who wouldn't jump to such a serious conclusion hastily. But she had seen nothing to suggest that this student was capable of writing such a paper. Fortunately, the paper had not been plagiarized, and I was able to offer her some background information that led her to see the student in a new light. He was one of the few people in his largely Latino Bronx neighborhood who was attending college. A shy student, we had nevertheless talked after class a few times, and he had shown me some curriculum work he had done for a tutoring program he was involved in. He was smart, thoughtful, and really engaged with the course material, but he was also nervous and, like many of our students, preoccupied with demands from his life outside of school. I can't be certain, of course, that this student, a Latino, felt comfortable sharing those aspects of his life with me because I am a first-generation Latina, but I would be surprised if that hadn't been a factor.

I'm suggesting that this is also an important point to bear in mind when thinking about higher education.

This brings us to my second point. We must pay attention to how we foster communities to which first-generation college students can feel connected, both in and out of the university classroom. This is not as easy or as automatic as it sounds. It is not enough to admit and hire a number of people whose parents didn't go to college. Take my institution, CCNY, as an example. In many ways, we do a fantastic job at providing an environment in which first-generation college students flourish. Raj Chetty's groundbreaking research on upward mobility shows that schools like CCNY do a much better job at moving students up the socio-economic ladder than the Ivy League schools, Stanford, Duke, and many other much wealthier educational institutions.[18] Some of this is simply numbers. We admit many more students from the lowest socioeconomic echelon than these other schools do. In 2015, 42 percent of the students that CUNY enrolled were first-generation college students; 38.5 percent were students whose families made less than $20,000 a year.[19] But it is equally important that those students feel that CUNY is a place for students like them. At City College's 2018 commencement, valedictorian Yasmine El Gheur, a first-generation college student and first-generation American, talked about the relief she felt upon arriving at CCNY after experiencing racism and ostracization for her Muslim background in upstate New York. El Gheur described how "it was not until I started school at my beloved City College, an institution that was formerly known as the Harvard of the poor, that I realized how much I had suppressed my identity, my heritage, to cope with my difference. . . . When I came to CCNY I felt like a weight had been lifted. For the first time in a long time I was surrounded by people who resembled me and who wanted to know the real me."[20] We don't fully understand the mechanisms by which schools like CCNY enable upward mobility, but the sentiment captured by El

18. Chetty et al., "Mobility Report Cards."
19. City University of New York, "Profile of Undergraduates."
20. El Gheur, "Commencement Address."

Gheur is surely a factor. Strivers look around and see a school that is meant to be for them.

Despite these successes, there are many ways in which my institution could do better. I hear from students who have a hard time finding a community at CCNY. More often than not, these students live at home. They travel from the far reaches of the five boroughs of New York City, often via multiple trains or buses, to get to campus. And once they arrive, they are thrust into crowded classrooms, sometimes led by poorly paid adjunct professors who are overwhelmed by the demands of teaching four or five courses just to get by. They sit and try to get as much as they can out of their lectures before they rush to another class and then back home or to work. I am fortunate that I still have the opportunity to teach smaller classes in which I can try my best to foster an inclusive community. I don't always succeed, but when I do, students learn as much or more from each other's diverse experiences as they do from me. I recently taught a class on philosophy of race in which I happened to have a handful of students from the Bronx who understood educational segregation, police brutality, and many of the other topics we covered in a visceral way. These students were brave and comfortable enough in our classroom to share their experiences, sometimes with tears in their eyes. After the class ended, many students told me how incredibly meaningful and impactful they had found the stories of their peers and how much reflection hearing those stories had prompted about their own lives.

Moments like this can feel magical, but there is no mystery in how they come about. The class I taught was small, around 23 students. I have dedicated myself to becoming a better teacher by learning more about pedagogy, even when at times it has conflicted with the demands of my research. I have been supported in my work by a generous salary and various grants that have enabled me to reduce my teaching load to a manageable amount. I am a woman of color and a first-generation college graduate. All educational institutions can invest in making this kind of experience a reality for more students by supporting smaller classes, by valuing teaching as much as research, by giving faculty a manageable course load, and by prioritizing inclusivity as part of their hiring criteria.

Between Hope and Hopelessness

The absence of discussion about the true costs of upward mobility forms the heart of the problem that confronts strivers. This silence is unsurprising. The vast majority of professors and administrators at CCNY and institutions like it are not themselves first-generation college graduates and thus have not experienced the particular challenges faced by the strivers for whom they are responsible. Some professors and administrators might simply be unaware of the full extent of the costs that strivers bear on the path of upward mobility. Others, I believe, have some sense of the magnitude of these costs but worry that they will seem condescending or presumptuous speaking about challenges with which they have little personal experience.

Another reason for our silence is even more basic and even less acknowledged: fear. We as educators are concerned that if students fully comprehend the extent of the challenges that they are taking on, many will be deterred from trying. This fear is probably warranted. My focus in this book has been on those students who succeed in overcoming these challenges, but they make up a small percentage of the students who are striving to get a college degree. Many more drop out at various points along that path. I suspect that many of these students do so because they encounter the challenges we have been discussing in this book and make different choices than those made by the strivers from whom we have heard. My conjecture is that if the path upward requires you to distance yourself from those aspects of your life that you find valuable in exchange for a very uncertain chance of "success," and if you come to see that these sacrifices are unfairly leveled on you because of an unjust and unequal distribution of opportunities and resources, it is not unreasonable to decide that you don't want to embark or continue on that path. Though I think that educators and parents should still aim to give students the best argument available in favor of college, the success of a student's path should not depend on hiding the truth from him or her.

The traditional story of upward mobility is an uplifting one. One cannot help but be inspired by Justice Sonia Sotomayor's journey from the Bronx through Princeton and Yale Law all the way to the Supreme Court.[21] If a Latina girl with diabetes raised by her widowed mother can make it by dint of hard work, maybe you can too. We prefer to focus on a story like hers, rather than that of her cousin Nelson, whom she describes as brighter than her, but who—while Sotomayor was prosecuting cases as a young lawyer—died from HIV after years of drug addiction. Sotomayor writes: "If I try to understand in my heart how it could happen that two children so closely matched could meet such different fates, I enter a subterranean world of nightmares—the sudden panic when Nelson's hand slips from mine in the press of the crowd, the monster I evade but he cannot."[22] The contrast in their fates is painful for Justice Sotomayor. And yet his story only makes it to us because we are drawn to hers—the story that offers hope and encourages us to think that our goals are within our reach if we work hard.

In her memoir, Justice Sotomayor is careful to note all of the people who helped her on her path and all of the sacrifices she had to make, including her marriage, in the service of her career. But we need not look at statistics to know that Justice Sotomayor's trajectory is exceptional. Most children who grow up like her will not end up climbing the ladder of opportunity nearly as far; many won't climb at all. We worry that this kind of honesty will lead to hopelessness—that if a high school kid from the Bronx recognizes that his fate is much more likely to be like Nelson's than Justice

---

21. Sotomayor, *My Beloved World*.
22. Sotomayor, *My Beloved World*, 253.

Sotomayor's, he will become dejected, cynical, and hopeless. That risk is real, but we cannot let it color our decisions. We cannot make hope the enemy of truth.

A beautiful example of this fine line between honesty and hopelessness is offered by Ta-Nehisi Coates's *Between the World and Me*. Written as a letter to his son, Coates's book doesn't pull any punches. He paints a historically rich, personal, and brutally honest portrait of the ways in which racism permeates the lives of all Americans. It is also a loving portrayal of the African American community in which Coates grew up. Yet the book was vehemently criticized, as much of Coates's work is, for articulating a vision of America that is bleak and hopeless. Melvin Rogers, in a powerful essay in the *Boston Review*, writes that the problem with Coates's work is that it portrays "the aspiration to defend a more exalted vision of this country's ethical and political life . . . as the hallmark of being asleep, dreaming in religious illusions. To be alive to an unvarnished reality, to be *woke*, is to recognize that no such country is possible."[23] The problem that many see at the heart of Coates's work is its fatalistic vision of America—one in which the legacy of racism determines the parameters of what is possible. Coates's response to this kind of criticism is that "a writer wedded to 'hope' is ultimately divorced from the 'truth.'"[24] But here Coates falls prey to the same problem that the peddlers of the story of upward mobility do—thinking that to have hope, one must turn a blind eye to the truth.

I have argued that we need to construct ethical narratives that are honest about the ethical costs of upward mobility, the necessity of trade-offs, the structural conditions that lead to those trade-offs, and how we can contribute to making things better once we have achieved a measure of success. Such narratives, I believe, are more honest than our typical narrative of upward mobility. This doesn't mean that they are less hopeful. To hope is not to believe

23. Rogers, "Keeping the Faith."
24. Coates, "Hope and the Historian."

against the evidence, but rather to see in what is before us the possibility for a better future.

For example, the fact that childcare is expensive and difficult to procure in this country means that some strivers find themselves having to choose between providing childcare for their families and graduating on time. A hopeless response to this situation would be to decide that such a striver will ultimately fail to graduate and therefore might as well not try. A delusionally optimistic response would be to encourage this striver to go to college and work hard to achieve her goals without acknowledging what she might be giving up by choosing that path. The ethical narrative, by contrast, points to a middle road: it helps the striver to acknowledge the potential ethical costs of going to college—how her relationship with her family might be impacted by the decisions she will have to make in order to succeed in that path—but also the potential gains—a college degree will enable her to access opportunities that are likely otherwise unavailable to her family. The ethical narrative also requires that she understand the ways in which a lack of access to quality childcare plays a role in the challenges she faces and how others who are born into more fortunate circumstances are not subject to the same challenges. This broadens her perspective. She can now consider the role she could play in bringing more quality childcare to people growing up in communities like hers once she has attained a measure of socioeconomic success. This contribution might be as simple as voting for candidates who make this one of their policy priorities, or it might involve a much more profound grassroots engagement with this issue. It is here that she can find hope not just for herself, but for others like her. Hope becomes more than an empty promise; it is born from an honest assessment of the challenges she faces and the sacrifices she will have to make. From the reflection at the heart of the ethical narrative, the striver can see her life more clearly. And from that clarity is born a more honest version of a hopeful narrative.

I am not suggesting that a clear-eyed ethical narrative will eliminate the feelings of conflict and struggle that strivers are liable to experience on the path of upward mobility, though some might take comfort from the clarity they have gained. Nor am I suggesting that this narrative will minimize the ethical costs strivers face, though it might help some thread the delicate needle between their two worlds. Nor am I suggesting that such a narrative would dramatically alter a striver's situation, though it may encourage strivers to act in ways that play a role in making our society more just in the long run. The reason to embrace a clear-eyed ethical narrative is simple—it is more honest. It is more truthful in its recognition that in the path of upward mobility there is the potential for loss, that what might be lost is genuinely valuable, and that the responsibility for that loss extends far beyond individual students, their families, or their communities.

Conclusion

MINIMIZING AND MITIGATING
ETHICAL COSTS

I have argued that in an unequal, socioeconomically segregated society like our own, strivers, as they travel the path of upward mobility, incur significant ethical costs for themselves, their families, and their communities. Those who grow up in communities in which disadvantages are concentrated must often seek opportunities for advancement elsewhere. If they succeed, their success in all likelihood will take them far from their families and communities. This distance will not just be literal. Strivers, in order to succeed, will have to prioritize their own path over important relationships, over obligations to their family, and over maintaining their ties to their community. In so doing, they risk sacrificing important and meaningful aspects of their lives and identities.

The story of the striver that I have been weaving throughout this book is an extreme version of the experience of upward mobility. Though we have met many real strivers whose stories bear some resemblance to this archetype, each striver has a unique experience of this phenomenon. Some are fortunate to incur fewer of the ethical costs we have discussed. Others return to their communities as teachers or social workers, or to start a business. Still others grow up not surrounded by poverty, but in middle-class communities. Furthermore, some middle-class and upper-middle-class students might end up relating to the striver's experience because of their own particular socioeconomic or family circumstances. A middle-class student whose family is thrown into financial chaos because of a medical emergency might end up struggling in many of the ways we have discussed. But it is strivers who are more likely to experience the tension between upward mobility and their ties to their families and communities as a result of the structural factors that disadvantage them. By relying on a stylized version of the striver's story, I have sought to bring the ethical aspect of the experience of upward mobility into sharp relief. But my hope is that each striver can find something in these pages that will help him or her more deeply understand his or her own unique experience of upward mobility.

It is also important that those who play critical roles in higher education—professors, administrators, and policymakers—recognize the ethical costs that students are bearing in order to improve their lives through education. Doing so deepens our dialogue about the many challenges currently facing the higher education sector. In this final chapter, I turn to considering how reflecting on ethical costs can enrich the perspectives of those who are charged with making policy decisions that affect the lives of strivers, whether these policies concern the broad shape of the higher education sector as a whole or specific exchanges happening within the classroom. In particular, I consider how a concern for minimizing and mitigating ethical costs might lead us to reconsider important issues in higher education. In the course of the discussion, I will touch on several examples—course requirements, classroom pedagogy, undermatching, and online education—that are topics of intense debate. While I am unable to give each of these discussions its full due here, I seek to show how taking the ethical perspective discussed in this book can fruitfully complicate those conversations.

Before we proceed, it is important to remember a point that I have made a number of times throughout this book. The higher education sector is very diverse, including technical schools, community colleges, for-profit professional schools, and Ivy League universities, among other institutions. I have focused in this book on strivers who have enrolled in a more "traditional" four-year college, but even here we find a huge variety. A university like mine that enrolls many minority and first-generation students is vastly different than an Ivy League university that enrolls a more privileged and Whiter student body and has the resources to spend more than twice as much on those students' education.[1] As I have stressed repeatedly, the ethical challenges students face differ depending on their own individual circumstances, but also depending on the institution in which they have enrolled. Consequently, even though in what follows I rely on some fairly broad claims, we must remain aware that the contours of each of these issues depend on the particular institution within which they play out.

Minimizing Ethical Costs

Many of the ethical costs that strivers experience would be minimized by changing the structural conditions that are largely responsible for them, but this rather obvious claim doesn't tell us much about what each of us as individuals can do. The reduction of poverty; the creation of a robust safety net that includes healthcare, daycare, and eldercare; and socioeconomic and racial integration of neighborhoods and schools are but a few of the rather massive structural changes that would be necessary to eliminate the challenges we have seen strivers confront throughout this book. This is not to say that in this utopian version of our society people wouldn't encounter ethical challenges and have to make difficult choices, but such choices would rarely involve choosing

---

1. Desrochers and Wellman, "Trends in College Spending 1998–2008."

their own individual flourishing at the expense of their communities' and families' wellbeing. In chapter 4, I argue that strivers have a special role to play in bringing about these structural changes. All of us, strivers and nonstrivers alike, can work toward transforming social structures in ways that minimize and equalize ethical costs. But those of us who work in higher education also have a special role to play in minimizing the ethical costs students bear even as these broader social structures remain frustratingly resistant to change.

Consider a recurring but seemingly banal feature of faculty and student life—course requirements. Every few years, faculty meet to discuss course requirements for majors or for their college as a whole. And every semester, students struggle to figure out how to fulfill these requirements. Course requirements serve a purpose—they make sure that students have a requisite baseline of knowledge and allow faculty members to teach more advanced courses that build on that knowledge base. But every requirement is potentially a hurdle to students' finishing their degrees on time and, depending on how frequently and at what times we offer a particular required course, can come into conflict with students' commitments to their families and communities.

My department had this conversation very recently. Some members of our faculty insisted that students should be required to take a certain number of core history courses. The problem is that these courses are only offered every other semester and, since they are usually taught by tenured faculty who are not inclined to want to teach over the weekend or at night, are taught during the day. This means that a student trying to finish a philosophy degree confronts a fairly inflexible set of requirements that might take him or her a long time to complete if he or she has to worry about a job, childcare, or a long commute home. Many of our students are in this situation. Of course, there were persuasive arguments in favor of the requirements as well. We want to ensure that a major from our department has some knowledge of a core of philosophical classics—Plato, Kant, and so on. But at what cost to the student?

Our department ultimately decided to cut one of the history requirements and offer students more flexibility, precisely because our chair brought up concerns about the costs we were imposing on our students. As a compromise, we decided that all senior faculty would try to include some of those historical classics in our regular upper-level courses. Our decision was motivated by awareness of the ethical costs that an additional set of rigid requirements would exact on our students. Of course, we are also limited in how much we can accommodate students' needs. Very few of us offer evening and weekend courses, though we do offer some, and not all of us can teach the required history course, so we cannot offer it as frequently as we would like. But considering the potential costs to important aspects of our students' lives allowed us to think more carefully about ways we might minimize those ethical costs for our students without seriously compromising their education. I don't mean to suggest that weighing the different factors at play in such a situation is easy or straightforward; rather, I aim to highlight that broadening the scope of the discussion allowed us to engage in a more thoughtful accounting of what was at stake in our decision.

The need for a broader conversation is true not only at the level of internal faculty debate, but also at the level of policy. For example, consider the recent discussion of undermatching—the phenomenon in which high-achieving, low-income students fail to apply to elite colleges and universities for which they are academically qualified despite the fact that they would get substantial financial aid from such schools. In fact, first-generation college students who attend well-funded private universities end up paying less for college and enjoying higher graduation rates than those who attend their local state school or community college.[2] Furthermore, the Ivy Leagues, Stanford, Notre Dame, and other universities with large endowments can offer students an incredible array of resources—counselors, writing centers, deans of student life, and so on—not to mention generous financial aid

2. Bowen et al., "Interactive Learning Online."

packages that can make the lives of strivers so much more manageable. Despite this, many low-income students do not apply to college at all, or if they do, they apply to institutions for which they are overqualified, often local community colleges or state schools.

Caroline Hoxby and Christopher Avery have done important work trying to better understand undermatching.[3] Certainly, as Hoxby and Avery argue, many students undermatch because they are not well informed about the college application process or the generous financial aid packages that are available at highly selective universities. Hoxby and Avery find that this is particularly true in parts of the country where such students might be isolated from other high-achieving students who are college bound or from mentors who have gone to selective institutions. But many of these students might not be applying because they want to remain close to family. Hoxby and Avery admit as much, but this passing consideration is not seriously explored in their research. Yet, as I have argued in this book, staying close to home is an important consideration for those strivers who are seeking to minimize the ethical costs that they will incur by seeking higher education. If we narrowly focus on the financial costs of this decision, we end up with a distorted picture of a striver's situation. When we also take the ethical costs into account, the decision-making of such students starts to seem less irrational or ill-informed.

Much of the literature on undermatching focuses on the phenomenon as a problem that needs to be fixed.[4] Hoxby, along with Sarah Turner, designed a very effective intervention that increased the number of high-achieving, low-income students who applied to college.[5] But again, little consideration has been paid in such studies to the ethical costs of this choice, not only for students, but for their communities. Of course, I do not mean to argue that we shouldn't engage in such interventions if they enable students

3. Hoxby and Avery, "Missing 'One-Offs.'"
4. For a thoughtful philosophical critique of this assumption, see Tiboris, "What's Wrong with Undermatching?"
5. Hoxby and Turner, "Expanding College Opportunities."

to go to institutions that will offer them more financial aid and increase their chances of graduation. But considering the ethical costs involved in going away to college might lead us to think about ways that we can help students minimize those costs. For example, some schools make trips back home a part of the financial aid package they offer low-income students. If we think through the issue of undermatching while keeping such factors in mind, we might arrive at other creative ways to minimize those often-overlooked ethical costs.

Mitigating Ethical Costs

Without reforming the social structures that are largely responsible for the disproportionate concentration of ethical costs on strivers, the extent to which we can *minimize* such costs is limited, but there is much we can do within the higher education sector to *mitigate* them. As I argue in chapter 1, the ethical costs in question cannot simply be redressed or offset by the financial or educational gains of a college education. For example, the community that an immigrant loses when he or she leaves home is not replaced by the new community that might be found in his or her new home. But finding this new community does go some way toward mitigating that loss. This is because gaining a community enriches the immigrant's life in a similar dimension to that in which the prior loss was incurred. An immigrant who has gained financially from immigrating but faces hostility in finding a community in his or her new home will have incurred a loss in his or her life that is unmitigated despite the financial gain. Mitigating ethical costs involves enriching students' lives in some of the dimensions in which they have been negatively impacted by the path of upward mobility. Colleges and universities can do little to mitigate the possible loss a striver might confront in his or her familial relationships, but they can offer a striver the opportunity to enter new communities and form new relationships.

Yet this is not as easy as it might seem. In the popular imagination, college is a time in students' lives when they easily enter into new friendships and relationships, but the reality is different for students from marginalized communities.[6] One reason is that many low-income students do not attend residential colleges, instead commuting to campus and perhaps living with family to reduce costs.[7] This limits the opportunities such students have to spontaneously interact with other students and faculty outside of the classroom. A second reason is that many strivers find college a difficult place to navigate, both culturally and socially. Remember Todd from chapter 1, who found it hard to make friends in college because he felt different from the other students there. His experience echoes what considerable research on first-generation and low-income students has established: these students tend to face greater challenges in making friends, connecting with professors, and finding a community on campus. As I illustrate in chapter 2, students who come from marginalized communities are more likely to encounter a cultural mismatch between the culture in which they grew up and the cultural frameworks that dominate colleges and universities.

These barriers to community mean that administrators and professors have to be more deliberate in taking steps to enable strivers to find those connections on campus. Consider, for example, what happens in the classroom. The standard college lecture in which a professor talks and 100 or so students sit and dutifully listen is not conducive to students developing relationships with each other. But professors have a lot of control not only over how they teach but also over how frequently and in what ways students interact with each other in their classroom. Thinking about mitigating the ethical costs strivers incur offers an opportunity for professors to rethink the classroom environment that they create. This is not to say that professors should think of the classroom as a place for students to socialize, but requiring students to engage in group projects, encouraging them to work on a problem set

6. I develop this argument more fully in Morton, "Mitigating Ethical Costs."
7. Sallie Mae and Ipsos Public Affairs, *How America Pays for College 2017*.

in pairs, or fostering a discussion-based class both is pedagogically effective and offers strivers more potential avenues into new friendships and communities. Strivers are much more likely than other students to feel "out of place" on campus, but a professor who manages his or her classroom with sensitivity and encourages student engagement can make it a place where strivers feel connected.

Finding the right balance between the various costs and benefits at stake for strivers is not always easy or straightforward. Take, for example, the case of online education. As we have seen, strivers facing serious ethical costs often need flexibility—to work, study, and invest the time they need in the relationships that matter to them. The rise of online degrees at for-profit schools such as the University of Phoenix and the adoption by many state universities, including my own, of online courses can be seen as a way for the higher education sector to offer such accommodation and minimize ethical costs.[8] This technology allows students to take courses from home whenever they are able to, freeing them up to spend time with their families or work. Such flexibility can also make it less burdensome for students to take required courses that might otherwise be oversubscribed or tough to fit into their schedules.

Unfortunately, as I have argued in other work, the more classes students take online, the more likely they are to miss out on a crucial part of the educational experience.[9] As we saw in chapter 2, one of the obstacles that strivers encounter in college is their unfamiliarity or discomfort with the norms that often prevail on a college campus, norms that are largely those of the college-educated middle and upper-middle class. Strivers, especially those who have grown up in communities in which disadvantage is concentrated, often discover a cultural gap at college that they need to learn to

---

8. There are various useful surveys of the current state of online education. See Allen and Seaman, "Changing Course"; Clinefelter and Magda, *Online Learning*; Bowen et al., "Interactive Learning Online"; and Jordan, "Initial Trends."

9. I develop this argument more fully in Morton, "Unequal Classrooms."

overcome. Socializing and interacting with middle-class professors, students, and administrators enables students to become adept at navigating the cultural frames that dominate not only the college campus, but also, crucially, the professional world. In so doing they learn how to join communities that are very different from their own. Students who miss out on that experience by not being on campus miss out on an important educational opportunity. Strivers, who have not grown up around those cultural frames, are the most liable to lose out by attempting to complete most of their education online.

The concern is not just that students are missing out on becoming familiar with the norms of middle-class educational institutions and workplaces, but that they will have fewer opportunities to develop the relationships that can go some way toward mitigating the ethical costs they might bear. Some students might prefer to minimize the financial and ethical costs they are liable to bear, even if they miss out on finding new communities and friendships. For some strivers, this is the right choice. A working mom who needs a college degree to get a promotion might reasonably prefer an online degree that minimizes her financial burden and ethical costs over spending time commuting to campus in order to find a new community there. But if we are thinking at the level of policy about online education as a way to increase upward mobility for low-income students, then we need to be careful about how we balance minimizing ethical costs and mitigating them and about how we communicate the true nature of these costs and benefits to students.

Of course, some online classrooms do allow students to build relationships and develop new social and cultural skills. Princeton University, for example, offers a series of online courses for low-income and first-generation first-year students who are unable to arrive on campus several weeks early for a series of classes and workshops designed specifically to help students like them prepare for the sort of challenges we have been discussing here.[10]

---

10. See https://access.princeton.edu/programs/fsi-2-u for more information.

These online classes have six to eight students per faculty member and an array of support staff. Students get to know their instructor and a handful of other students quite well and can use those relationships as building blocks for creating a community on campus once they arrive. This is an extraordinary use of online education, but it is not a model that could be easily scaled up to lower costs or to serve much larger numbers of students, as would likely be necessary at the kinds of institutions that most strivers are attending.

Online education can play a critical role in minimizing financial and ethical costs, but in many cases, this will come at the expense of strivers developing important cultural competencies, finding opportunities to build new relationships, and entering new communities. There is much more to be said here, but suffice it to say that thinking about ethical costs can enrich our conversation about whether online education can be a cost-effective vehicle in the journey toward upward mobility.

Beyond Strivers

Though in this book we have focused on understanding the ethical costs of upward mobility, it's important to reiterate that there are many gains that strivers and their families experience as a result of the striver's success. In the best case, strivers who have gained a college education have enriched their lives in a number of ways. They have gained critical skills and knowledge, degrees that can open doors to interesting and well-paying careers, new relationships, and new perspectives on the surrounding world. In many cases, family members also benefit from a striver's improved financial position, acquired knowledge and skills, and elevated social class. In some cases, communities also stand to gain. That striver might provide mentorship, serve as an example to others in the community, or act as a connection to a different, more affluent community. And, of course, families and communities feel pride at seeing what one of theirs has accomplished. It is for all this that strivers sacrifice.

However, as I have repeatedly urged throughout this book, we must remember that ethical costs are borne not just by strivers, but by those around them—parents, friends, and community. This is another way in which the discussion around higher education could be less myopic. We need to start talking about the costs of college for those families and communities who send young people to college. In the course of my research, I have spoken with many strivers, without whose willingness to share their experiences and insights I could never have completed this book. Yet the more I discover about the experiences of strivers, the more questions I am left with—not about the strivers, but about their parents, friends, and communities. I want to know: What costs, financial and ethical, are they bearing in sending a child off to college? How are they making sense of these costs? What benefits do they see themselves as having received? What kind of ethical trade-offs are they making? These are questions for future research, but I hope that this book has also provoked you to ask them, because just as the debate on higher education focuses too narrowly on financial costs, it also focuses too narrowly on the student as an individual.

Many see higher education as the way to enable children to lead rich, flourishing adult lives. Parents, teachers, friends, and neighbors invest energy in the children under their care with this hope. But we must remember that individuals lead lives in community with others. Much of the meaning in our lives is derived from our relationships with those around us. Yet because of the ways in which opportunity is distributed in this country, those ties can become liabilities for individuals born into disadvantage, at odds with their own individual flourishing. Higher education should not be seen just as a benefit for the student who goes to college. It should also be understood as a way to enrich the lives of the student's community as well. For disadvantaged communities, that promise too often remains unfulfilled.

BIBLIOGRAPHY

Ainsworth-Darnell, James W., and Douglas B Downey. "Assessing the Oppositional Culture Explanation for Racial/Ethnic Differences in School Performance." *American Sociological Review* 63, no. 4 (1998): 536–553. https://doi.org/10.2307/2657266.

Allen, I. Elaine, and Jeff Seaman. "Changing Course: Ten Years of Tracking Online Education in the United States." Babson Survey Research Group (2013). https://www.onlinelearningsurvey.com/reports/changingcourse.pdf.

American Academy of Arts & Sciences. "Racial/Ethnic Distribution of Degrees in Philosophy." Humanities Indicators (2016). https://www.humanitiesindicators.org/content/indicatordoc.aspx?i=266.

Anderson, Elizabeth. "Fair Opportunity in Education: A Democratic Perspective." *Ethics* 117, no. 4 (July 2007): 595–622.

———. *The Imperative of Integration.* Princeton, NJ: Princeton University Press, 2010.

Appiah, K. Anthony. "Race, Culture, Identity: Misunderstood Connections." Tanner Lectures on Human Values, University of California, San Diego, October 27–28, 1994.

Aristotle. "The Nichomachean Ethics." Translated by W. D. Ross. In *Complete Works of Aristotle*, vol. 2: *The Revised Oxford Translation*, ed. Jonathan Barnes, 1729–1867. Princeton, NJ: Princeton University Press, 1984.

———. "Politics." Translated by B. Jowett. In *Complete Works of Aristotle*, vol. 2: *The Revised Oxford Translation*, ed. Jonathan Barnes, 1986–2129. Princeton, NJ: Princeton University Press, 1984.

Armstrong, Elizabeth A., and Laura T. Hamilton. *Paying for the Party.* Cambridge, MA: Harvard University Press, 2013.

Aud, Susan, William Hussar, Michael Planty, Thomas Snyder, Kevin Bianco, Mary Ann Fox, Lauren Frohlich, Jana Kemp, and Lauren Drake. "The Condition of Education 2010." NCES 2010–028. National Center for Education Statistics (2010). https://nces.ed.gov/pubs2010/2010028.pdf.

Bailey, Martha J., and Susan M. Dynarski. "Inequality in Postsecondary Education." In *Whither Opportunity?: Rising Inequality, Schools, and Children's Life Chances*, ed. Greg J Duncan and Richard J. Murnane, 117–132. New York: Russell Sage Foundation, 2011.

Beam, Christopher. "Code Black." *Slate*, January 11, 2010. http://www.slate.com/articles/news_and_politics/politics/2010/01/code_black.html.

Beasley, Maya A. *Opting Out: Losing the Potential of America's Young Black Elite.* Chicago: University of Chicago Press, 2012.

Benet-Martínez, Verónica, Janxin Leu, Fiona Lee, and Michael W. Morris. "Negotiating Biculturalism Cultural Frame Switching in Biculturals with Oppositional Versus Compatible Cultural Identities." *Journal of Cross-Cultural Psychology* 33, no. 5 (2002): 492–516.

Bertrand, Marianne, and Sendhil Mullainathan. "Are Emily and Greg More Employable Than Lakisha and Jamal?: A Field Experiment on Labor Market Discrimination." *American Economic Review* 94, no. 4 (2004): 991–1013.

Bowen, William G., Matthew M. Chingos, Kelly A. Lack, and Thomas I. Nygren. "Interactive Learning Online at Public Universities: Evidence from a Six-Campus Randomized Trial." *Journal of Policy Analysis and Management* 33, no. 1 (2014): 94–111.

Bowen, William G., Matthew M. Chingos, and Michael S. McPherson. *Crossing the Finish Line: Completing College at America's Public Universities.* Princeton, NJ: Princeton University Press, 2009.

Bowen, William G., and Michael S. McPherson. *Lesson Plan: An Agenda for Change in American Higher Education.* Princeton, NJ: Princeton University Press, 2016.

Bowles, Samuel, Herbert Gintis, and Melissa Osborne-Graves, eds. *Unequal Chances: Family Background and Economic Success.* Princeton, NJ: Princeton University Press, 2005.

Bretherton, Inge. "The Origins of Attachment Theory: John Bowlby and Mary Ainsworth." *Developmental Psychology* 28, no. 5 (1992): 759–775. https://psycnet.apa.org/doi/10.1037/0012-1649.28.5.759.

Brighouse, Harry, and Adam Swift. *Family Values: The Ethics of Parent-Child Relationships.* Princeton, NJ: Princeton University Press, 2014.

Bureau of Labor Statistics. "Unemployment Rates and Earnings by Educational Attainment" (2017). https://www.bls.gov/emp/tables/unemployment-earnings-education.htm.

Butt, Daniel. "On Benefiting from Injustice." *Canadian Journal of Philosophy* 37, no. 1 (2007): 129–152.

Cahalan, Margaret, Laura Perna, Mika Yamashita, Roman Ruiz, and Khadish Franklin. "Indicators of Higher Education Equity in the United States: 2016 Historical Trend Report." Pell Institute for the Study of Opportunity in Higher Education (2016). http://pellinstitute.org/downloads/publications-Indicators_of_Higher_Education_Equity_in_the_US_2016_Historical_Trend_Report.pdf.

Carter, Prudence. *Keepin' It Real: School Success Beyond Black and White.* Cambridge: Oxford University Press, 2005.

Chang, Ruth. "Are Hard Choices Cases of Incomparability?" *Philosophical Issues* 22, no. 1 (2012): 106–126.

———. "How to Make Hard Choices." TED Salon New York, 14:38. May 2014. https://www.ted.com/talks/ruth_chang_how_to_make_hard_choices.

Chetty, Raj, Nathaniel Hendren, Patrick Kline, and Emmanuel Saez. "Where Is the Land of Opportunity?: The Geography of Intergenerational Mobility in the United

States." *Quarterly Journal of Economics* 129, no. 4 (2014): 1553–1623. https://doi
.org/10.1093/qje/qju022.

Chetty, Raj, John N. Friedman, Emmanuel Saez, Nicholas Turner, and Danny Yagan.
"Mobility Report Cards: The Role of Colleges in Intergenerational Mobility."
NBER Working Paper No. 23618 (July 2017). http://www.equality-of-opportunity
.org/assets/documents/coll_mrc_summary.pdf.

Chetty, Raj, Nathaniel Hendren, Patrick Kline, Emmanuel Saez, and Nicholas Turner.
"Is the United States Still a Land of Opportunity?: Recent Trends in Intergenerational Mobility." *American Economic Review* 104, no. 5 (2014): 141–147.

City College of New York. "About Us." https://giving.ccny.cuny.edu/about-us.

City University of New York. "A Profile of Undergraduates at CUNY Senior and Community Colleges." Office of Institutional Research and Assessment (Fall 2015).
http://www2.cuny.edu/wp-content/uploads/sites/4/media-assets/ug_student
_profile_f15.pdf.

Clinefelter, David L., and Andrew J. Magda. *Online Learning at Private Colleges and Universities: A Survey of Chief Academic Officers.* Louisville, KY: Learning House, 2013.

Coates, Ta-Nehisi. *Between the World and Me.* New York: Spiegel & Grau, 2015.

———. "The Case for Reparations." *Atlantic* 313, no. 5 (2014): 54–71.

———. "Hope and the Historian." *Atlantic*, December 10, 2015. http://www.theatlantic
.com/politics/archive/2015/12/hope-and-the-historian/419961.

Cohen, G. A. "Rescuing Conservatism: A Defense of Existing Value." In *Finding Oneself
in the Other*, ed. Michael Otsuka, 143–174. Princeton, NJ: Princeton University
Press, 2012.

Cohen, Geoffrey L., and Julio Garcia. "'I Am Us': Negative Stereotypes as Collective
Threats." *Journal of Personality and Social Psychology* 89, no. 4 (2005): 566–582.

Cohen, Geoffrey L., Julio Garcia, Valerie Purdie-Vaughns, Nancy Apfel, and Patricia
Brzustoski. "Recursive Processes in Self-Affirmation: Intervening to Close the
Minority Achievement Gap." *Science* 324, no. 5925 (2009): 400–403.

Cohen, Geoffrey L., and David K. Sherman. "The Psychology of Change: Self-
Affirmation and Social Psychological Intervention." *Annual Review of Psychology*
65 (2014): 333–371.

Collins, Caitlyn. "The Real Mommy War Is Against the State." *New York Times*, Feb-
ruary 9, 2019. https://www.nytimes.com/2019/02/09/opinion/sunday/the-real
-mommy-war-is-against-the-state.html.

Dawsey, Josh. "Trump Derides Protections for Immigrants from 'Shithole' Countries."
Washington Post, January 12, 2018. https://www.washingtonpost.com/politics
/trump-attacks-protections-for-immigrants-from-shithole-countries-in-oval
-office-meeting/2018/01/11/bfc0725c-f711-11e7-91af-31ac729add94_story.html.

Delpit, Lisa D. *Other People's Children: Cultural Conflict in the Classroom.* New York:
New Press, 1995.

Dennett, Daniel C. "The Self as a Center of Narrative Gravity." In *Self and Consciousness:
Multiple Perspectives*, ed. Frank S. Kessel, Pamela M. Cole, Dale L. Johnson, and
Milton D. Hakel, 111–123. New York: Psychology Press, 1992.

Desrochers, Donna M., and Jane V. Wellman. "Trends in College Spending 1998–2008: Where Does the Money Come From? Where Does It Go? What Does It Buy?" Delta Project on Postsecondary Education Costs, Productivity, and Accountability (2011). https://files.eric.ed.gov/fulltext/ED539420.pdf.

Du Bois, W. E. Burghardt. "Strivings of the Negro People." *Atlantic*, August 1897. https://www.theatlantic.com/magazine/archive/1897/08/strivings-of-the-negro-people/305446.

Duncan, Greg J., and Richard J. Murnane, eds. *Whither Opportunity?: Rising Inequality, Schools, and Children's Life Chances*. New York: Russell Sage Foundation, 2011.

El Gheur, Yasmine. "Commencement Address." Speech delivered at the 2018 City College of New York Commencement, New York, June 1, 2018. https://www.youtube.com/watch?v=3_bAve9vbcQ.

Espinoza, Roberta. "The Good Daughter Dilemma: Latinas Managing Family and School Demands." *Journal of Hispanic Higher Education* 9, no. 4 (2010): 317–330.

Feinberg, Joel. "The Child's Right to an Open Future." In *Philosophy of Education: An Anthology*, ed. Randall Curren, 112–123. Oxford: Blackwell, 2007.

Fordham, Signithia, and John U. Ogbu. "Black Students' School Success: Coping with the Burden of 'Acting White.'" *Urban Review* 18, no. 3 (1986): 176–206.

Frankfurt, Harry G. *The Reasons of Love*. Princeton, NJ: Princeton University Press, 2004.

Fuligni, Andrew J., and Sara Pedersen. "Family Obligation and the Transition to Young Adulthood." *Developmental Psychology* 38, no. 5 (2002): 856–868. http://dx.doi.org/10.1037/0012-1649.38.5.856.

Goffman, Erving. *The Presentation of Self in Everyday Life*. New York: Doubleday, 1959.

Goldrick-Rab, Sara. *Paying the Price: College Costs, Financial Aid, and the Betrayal of the American Dream*. London: University of Chicago Press, 2016.

Goldrick-Rab, Sara, and Nancy Kendall. "The Real Price of College." Century Foundation Report, March 3, 2016. https://tcf.org/content/report/the-real-price-of-college/.

Gopnik, Allison, Andrew N. Meltzoff, and Patricia K. Kuhl. *The Scientist in the Crib: What Early Learning Tells Us About the Mind*. New York: Harper Collins, 1999.

Harackiewicz, Judith M., Elizabeth A. Canning, Yoi Tibbetts, Cynthia J. Giffen, Seth S. Blair, Douglas I. Rouse, and Janet S. Hyde. "Closing the Social Class Achievement Gap for First-Generation Students in Undergraduate Biology." *Journal of Educational Psychology* 106, no. 2 (2014): 375–389.

Haslanger, Sally. "Gender and Race: (What) Are They? (What) Do We Want Them to Be?" *Noûs* 34, no. 1 (2000): 31–55.

Hochschild, Arlie Russell. *The Managed Heart: Commercialization of Human Feeling*. Berkeley: University of California Press, 1983.

Hoxby, Caroline, and Christopher Avery. "The Missing 'One-Offs': The Hidden Supply of High-Achieving, Low-Income Students." *Brookings Papers on Economic Activity*, no. 1 (2013): 1–65. https://doi.org/10.1353/eca.2013.0000.

Hoxby, Caroline, and Sarah Turner. "Expanding College Opportunities for High-Achieving, Low Income Students." SIEPR Discussion Paper No. 12–014. Stanford

Institute for Economic Policy Research (2013). https://siepr.stanford.edu/sites
/default/files/publications/12-014paper_6.pdf.

Isaacson, Walter. *Steve Jobs*. New York: Simon & Schuster, 2011.

Jack, Anthony Abraham. "Crisscrossing Boundaries: Variation in Experiences with
Class Marginality among Lower-Income, Black Undergraduates at an Elite College." In *College Students' Experiences of Power and Marginality: Sharing Spaces
and Negotiating Differences*, ed. Elizabeth M. Lee and Chaise LaDousa, 83–101.
New York: Routledge, 2015.

———. "Culture Shock Revisited: The Social and Cultural Contingencies to Class
Marginality." *Sociological Forum* 29, no. 2 (2014): 453–475. https://www.jstor.org
/stable/43654103.

———. "(No) Harm in Asking: Class, Acquired Cultural Capital, and Academic
Engagement at an Elite University." *Sociology of Education* 89, no. 1 (2015): 1–19.
https://doi.org/10.1177%2F0038040715614913.

Jensen, Barbara. *Reading Classes: On Culture and Classism in America*. New York: Cornell University Press, 2012.

Jollimore, Troy. *Love's Vision*. Princeton, NJ: Princeton University Press, 2011.

Jordan, Katy. "Initial Trends in Enrolment and Completion of Massive Open Online
Courses." *International Review of Research in Open and Distributed Learning* 15,
no. 1 (2014). https://doi.org/10.19173/irrodl.v15i1.1651.

Khan, Shamus Rahman. *Privilege: The Making of an Adolescent Elite at St. Paul's School*.
Princeton, NJ: Princeton University Press, 2010.

Klein, Ezra. "Understanding Hillary: Why the Clinton America Sees Isn't the Clinton
the Colleagues Know." *Vox*, July 11, 2016. http://www.vox.com/a/hillary-clinton
-interview/the-gap-listener-leadership-quality.

Kraus, Michael W., and Jacinth J. X. Tan. "Americans Overestimate Social Class Mobility." *Journal of Experimental Social Psychology* 58 (2015): 101–111. https://doi.org
/10.1016/j.jesp.2015.01.005.

LaFromboise, Teresa, Hardin L. K. Coleman, and Jennifer Gerton. "Psychological
Impact of Biculturalism: Evidence and Theory." *Psychological Bulletin* 114, no. 3
(1993): 395–412. https://psycnet.apa.org/doi/10.1037/0033-2909.114.3.395.

Lareau, Annette. *Unequal Childhoods: Class, Race, and Family Life*. Berkeley: University of California Press, 2003.

Levinson, Meira. *No Citizen Left Behind*. Cambridge, MA: Harvard University Press,
2012.

MacIntyre, Alasdair. *After Virtue: A Study in Moral Theory*. Notre Dame, IN: University
of Notre Dame Press, 1984.

Markus, Hazel Rose, and Shinobu Kitayama. "Culture and the Self: Implications for Cog-
nition, Emotion, and Motivation." *Psychological Review* 98, no. 2 (1991): 224–253.

Mill, John Stuart. "Inaugural Address Delivered to the University of St. Andrews,
Feb. 1st, 1867." In *Classic and Contemporary Readings in the Philosophy of Education*, ed. Steven M. Cahn, 185–210. New York: Oxford University Press, 2011.

Mills, Charles W. "Racial Liberalism." In *Black Rights/White Wrongs: The Critique of
Racial Liberalism*, 49–71. Oxford: Oxford University Press, 2017.

BIBLIOGRAPHY

Mishel, Lawrence, Josh Bivens, Elise Gould, and Heidi Shierholz. *The State of Working America*. New York: Cornell University Press, 2012.

Morton, Jennifer M. "An Antidote to Injustice." *Philosophers' Magazine*, no. 69 (2015): 65–70.

———. "Cultural Code-Switching: Straddling the Achievement Gap." *Journal of Political Philosophy* 22, no. 3 (2013): 259–281. http://dx.doi.org/10.1111/jopp.12019.

———. "Mitigating Ethical Costs in the Classroom." *Daedalus: Journal of the American Academy of Arts and Sciences* (forthcoming).

———. "Unequal Classrooms: Online Higher Education and Non-Cognitive Skills." *Philosophical Inquiry in Education* 23, no. 2 (2016): 97–113.

Nguyen, Angela-MinhTu D., and Verónica Benet-Martínez. "Biculturalism Unpacked: Components, Measurement, Individual Differences, and Outcomes." *Social and Personality Psychology Compass* 1, no. 1 (2007): 101–114. https://doi.org/10.1111/j.1751-9004.2007.00029.x.

Noggle, Robert. "Special Agents: Children's Autonomy and Parental Authority." In *The Moral and Political Status of Children*, ed. David Archard and Colin M. Macleod, 97–117. Oxford: Oxford University Press, 2002.

Obama, Barack. *Dreams from My Father: A Story of Race and Inheritance*. New York: Three Rivers Press, 2004.

Okin, Susan Moller, Joshua Cohen, Matthew Howard, and Martha Craven Nussbaum. *Is Multiculturalism Bad for Women?* Princeton, NJ: Princeton University Press, 1999.

Orfield, Gary, Mark D. Bachmeier, David R. James, and Tamela Eitle. "Deepening Segregation in American Public Schools: A Special Report from the Harvard Project on School Desegregation." *Equity and Excellence in Education* 30, no. 2 (1997): 5–24.

Orfield, Gary, John Kucsera, and Genevieve Siegel-Hawley. "E Pluribus . . . Separation: Deepening Double Segregation for More Students." Civil Rights Project/Proyecto Derechos Civiles (2012). https://escholarship.org/uc/item/8g58m2v9.

Padilla, Amado M. "Bicultural Social Development." *Hispanic Journal of Behavioral Sciences* 28, no. 4 (2006): 467–497. https://doi.org/10.1177/0739986306294255.

Parker, Ian. "The Gift." *New Yorker*, August 2, 2004, 54–63.

Patterson, Orlando, and Jacqueline Rivers. "'Try on the Outfit and Just See How It Works': The Psychocultural Responses of Disconnected Youth to Work." In *The Cultural Matrix: Understanding Black Youth*, ed. Orlando Patterson and Ethan Fosse, 415–43. Cambridge, MA: Harvard University Press, 2015.

Pew Research Center. "Sharp Partisan Divisions in Views of National Institutions" (July 2017). http://www.people-press.org/wp-content/uploads/sites/4/2017/07/07-10-17-Institutions-release.pdf.

———. "The State of American Jobs: How the Shifting Economic Landscape Is Reshaping Work and Society and Affecting the Way People Think about the Skills and Training They Need to Get Ahead" (October 2016). http://assets.pewresearch.org/wp-content/uploads/sites/3/2016/10/ST_2016.10.06_Future-of-Work_FINAL4.pdf.

Phillips, L. Taylor, Nicole M. Stephens, Sarah S. Townsend, and Sébastien Goudeau. "Access Is Not Enough: Cultural Mismatch Persists to Limit First-Generation Students' Opportunities for Achievement Throughout College." http://www .nicolemstephens.com/uploads/3/9/5/9/39596235/accessisnotenough_final.pdf.

Piketty, Thomas. *Capital in the Twenty-First Century*. Trans. Arthur Goldhammer. Cambridge: Belknap Press of Harvard University Press, 2013.

Pinsker, Joe. "Rich Kids Study English." *Atlantic*, July 6, 2015. https://www.theatlantic .com/business/archive/2015/07/college-major-rich-families-liberal-arts/397439/.

Plato. "Republic." Trans. G.M.A. Grube. In *Plato: Complete Works*, ed. John M. Cooper, 971–1223. Indianapolis, IN: Hackett, 1997.

Rivera, Lauren A. *Pedigree: How Elite Students Get Elite Jobs*. Princeton, NJ: Princeton University Press, 2015.

Rogers, Melvin. "Keeping the Faith." *Boston Review*, November 1, 2017. http:// bostonreview.net/race/melvin-rogers-keeping-faith.

Rumore, Kori. "Trump on Chicago: 'A Disaster' 'Out of Control,' 'Not Good!' . . . 'It's a Great City.'" *Chicago Tribune*, October 8, 2018. http://www.chicagotribune.com /news/local/breaking/ct-trump-tweets-quotes-chicago-htmlstory.html.

Sallie Mae and Ipsos Public Affairs. *How America Pays for College 2017*. Washington, D.C.: Sallie Mae, 2017. https://www.salliemae.com/assets/Research/HAP /HowAmericaPaysforCollege2017.pdf.

Schechtman, Marya. *The Constitution of Selves*. Ithaca, NY: Cornell University Press, 2007.

Scheffler, Samuel. *Boundaries and Allegiances: Problems of Justice and Responsibility in Liberal Thought*. Oxford: Oxford University Press, 2002.

———. "Morality and Reasonable Partiality." In *Partiality and Impartiality: Morality, Special Relationships, and the Wider World*, ed. Brian Feltham and John Cottingham, 98–130. Oxford: Oxford University Press, 2010.

———. "Valuing." In *Reasons and Recognition: Essays on the Philosophy of T. M. Scanlon*, ed. R. Jay Wallace, Rahul Kumar, and Samuel Freeman, 23–42. Oxford: Oxford University Press, 2011.

Sennett, Richard, and Jonathan Cobb. *The Hidden Injuries of Class*. New York: Vintage, 1973.

Singer, Peter. "Famine, Affluence, and Morality." *Philosophy & Public Affairs* 1, no. 3 (1972): 229–243. https://www.jstor.org/stable/2265052.

Smirnensky, Hristo. "The Tale of the Stairs." In *Selected Poetry and Prose*, trans. Peter Tempest, 140–142. Sofia: Sofia Press, 1980.

Sotomayor, Sonia. *My Beloved World*. New York: Vintage, 2013.

Stephens, Nicole M., Stephanie A. Fryberg, Hazel Rose Markus, Camille S. Johnson, and Rebecca Covarrubias. "Unseen Disadvantage: How American Universities' Focus on Independence Undermines the Academic Performance of First-Generation College Students." *Journal of Personality and Social Psychology* 102, no. 6 (2012): 1178–1197. https://doi.org/10.1037/a0027143.

Stephens, Nicole M., MarYam G. Hamedani, and Mesmin Destin. "Closing the Social-Class Achievement Gap: A Difference-Education Intervention Improves

First-Generation Students' Academic Performance and All Students' College Transition." *Psychological Science* 25, no. 4 (2014): 943–953. https://doi.org/10 .1177/0956797613518349.

Swidler, Ann. "Culture in Action: Symbols and Strategies." *American Sociological Review* 51, no. 2 (1986): 273–286. https://doi.org/10.2307/2095521.

Sy, Susan R., and Jessica Romero. "Family Responsibilities among Latina College Students from Immigrant Families." *Journal of Hispanic Higher Education* 7, no. 3 (2008): 212–227. https://doi.org/10.1177/1538192708316208.

Taylor, Charles. *Sources of the Self: The Making of the Modern Identity.* Cambridge, MA: Harvard University Press, 1989.

Tiboris, Michael. "What's Wrong with Undermatching?" *Journal of Philosophy of Education* 48, no. 4 (2014): 646–664. https://doi.org/10.1111/1467-9752.12091.

Tinto, Vincent. "Taking Retention Seriously: Rethinking the First Year of College." *NACADA Journal* 19, no. 2 (1999): 5–9. https://doi.org/10.12930/0271-9517-19.2.5.

Torrey, E. Fuller. "Jails and Prisons—America's New Mental Hospitals." *American Journal of Public Health* 85, no. 12 (1995): 1611–1613.

Trustees of Princeton University. *Report of the Task Force on Relationships Between the University and the Eating Clubs.* Princeton University (2010). http://wayback .archive-it.org/5151/20180103094438/http://www.princeton.edu/reports/2010 /ectf/docs/ECTF_Report.pdf.

Tyson, Karolyn, William Darity, and Domini R. Castellino. "It's Not 'a Black Thing': Understanding the Burden of Acting White and Other Dilemmas of High Achievement." *American Sociological Review* 70, no. 4 (2005): 582–605. https://doi.org /10.1177/000312240507000403.

United Nations. "Sharp Increase in Money Migrants Send Home Lifts Millions out of Poverty." United Nations News Centre, June 14, 2017. http://www.un.org/apps /news/story.asp?NewsID=56973.

Velleman, J. David. *How We Get Along.* Cambridge: Cambridge University Press, 2009.

Whittaker, Richard. "Johnston High School Is Dead; Long Live . . . ?" *Austin Chronicle,* July 4, 2008. https://www.austinchronicle.com/news/2008-07-04/641755.

Williams, Bernard Arthur Owen. *Ethics and the Limits of Philosophy.* Cambridge, MA: Harvard University Press, 1986.

Wilson, Timothy D., Michelle Damiani, and Nicole Shelton. "Improving the Academic Performance of College Students with Brief Attributional Interventions." In *Improving Academic Achievement,* ed. Joshua Aronson, 89–108. San Diego: Elsevier, 2002. https://doi.org/10.1016/B978-012064455-1/50008-7.

Wolff, Edward N. "Household Wealth Trends in the United States, 1962 to 2013: What Happened over the Great Recession?" *RSF: The Russell Sage Foundation Journal of the Social Sciences* 2, no. 6 (2016): 24–43.

Young, Iris Marion. *Responsibility for Justice.* Oxford: Oxford University Press, 2010.

Zheng, Robin. "What Is My Role in Changing the System?: A New Model of Responsibility for Structural Injustice." *Ethical Theory and Moral Practice* 21, no. 4 (2018): 869–885. https://doi.org/10.1007/s10677-018-9892-8.

INDEX

A NOTE ON THE TYPE

This book has been composed in Adobe Text and Gotham.
Adobe Text, designed by Robert Slimbach for Adobe,
bridges the gap between fifteenth- and sixteenth-century
calligraphic and eighteenth-century Modern styles.
Gotham, inspired by New York street signs, was designed
by Tobias Frere-Jones for Hoefler & Co.